ABOUT HER

ABOUT HER

Stories of Grace, Grit, Grievance, and Gratitude

Edited by Josephine Carubia and Michele Glorie Palmer

Copyright © 2011 by Metaphorical Ink.
Introduction and editorial material by Josephine Carubia and Michele Glorie Palmer.
Copyright of individual stories is held by each author.

Published by
Metaphorical Ink
330 East Irvin Avenue
State College, PA 16801
www.metaphorical-ink.com

All rights reserved. No part of this publication may be reproduced in any form or by any means, electronic or mechanical, including photocopying, recording, or by any information storage and retrieval system, without permission in writing from the publisher and authors. All inquiries should be addressed to Metaphorical Ink, 330 East Irvin Avenue, State College, PA 16801.

Acknowledgements

"Driving to the Beach" © 2009 by Claire Aldrich. "Great Aunt Plenty and Great Aunt Peace" is an excerpt from pages 1-3 of Eight Cousins, or, The Aunt-Hill by Louisa May Alcott. © 1874 Louisa May Alcott. 1876, Roberts Brothers, Boston. Google digitized book from Harvard University Library. Public domain. "Sweet Haven" is an excerpt from the poem "Out to Old Aunt Mary's" by James Whitcomb Riley. 1904: The Bobbs-Merrill Company. Google digitized books. Public domain. Previously published in Women in the Family: A Custom Memory Album edited by Josephine Carubia and Michele Glorie Palmer. 2001: Boundless Net Handmade Books, State College, PA. "Layer by Layer," "Gramma and Barbie," "On the Road," "Hurricane Bob Salad," "You Were There," "I Married a Mother." Used by permission of the authors and editors. "Mother Cora" by Paul Bixby is previously published in Vol. XIII, No. 3, Summer 2009, pp. 8-9 of Foxdale Miscellany. Used by permission of the author and editor.

Printed by K-B Offset Printing, Inc. / theprinters.com

First Edition April 2011

Cover and interior design by Ken Volk
www.lilkennydesign.com

ISBN: 978-0-9833250-0-0

To Anna, Teah, Dakota, Givanni, Treyton, Milanni, and a new generation of storytellers

Table of Contents

INTRODUCTION 1

SECTION ONE — THE VIEW OF A CHILD 5
   Heaven Beneath Her Feet, Michael Azevedo   6
   Early Morning at Roundfield, Juliet Silveri   8
   The Folder, Susan Bordo   10
   Saved by an Angel, Joseph D'Ambrosio   12
   A Twelve-year-old Girl, Hoasua   14
   Gramma and Barbie, Taryn Snyder   16
   Life and Death, Anne Allan Whitney   18
   Marks of Our Labors, Shel Julian Kessel   20

SECTION TWO — LIFE'S JOURNEYS 21
   Driving to the Beach, Claire Aldrich   22
   On the Road, Andrea Pinto Lebowitz   25
   A Baseball Story, Lisa L. Courcy   28
   Dove, Kim McNamara   30
   Priorities, Miguelina (Millie) Santana   32
   Too Independent, Alpa Patel   34
   Mapping Love, Nancy Tuana   36
   Our Last Road Trip, Laura Souza   37

SECTION THREE — SNAPSHOTS, PHOTOGRAPHS, AND PORTRAITS 41
   Unpacking, Gabeba Baderoon   42
   Tomato Soup ... A Silver Moon, Cindy Carubia   44
   Reflections on a Life Well Lived, Joanne Balmer Green   46
   An Irish Lady, Annette Conklin   47
   My Mother's Flesh, Josephine Carubia   50
   My Mother as a Woman, Robert E. Innis   51

SECTION FOUR — THE GREAT AND THE GRAND 53
   Flora, Laurie Mansell Reich   54
   Sweet Haven, James Whitcomb Riley   58
   Optimism, Marina Berges   59
   Generations, Roslynne Canfield   62
   Haantje: Johanna Johansson van den Berge, Elizabeth Vozzola   66
   Inspiration, Suzanne (Sica) Bokenko   70
   A Mother's Heart, Hyo Kim   72
   Great Aunt Plenty and Great Aunt Peace, Louisa M. Alcott   74
   Bunia, Elzbieta Sikora   75

SECTION FIVE — THREADS AND THEMES AND TIES THAT BIND US 79
- *Kimono Threads*, Mizuho Kawasaki — 80
- *A Stitch of Time*, Liz Maroney — 82
- *Resemblance*, Laura de Kreij — 84
- *Cossacks*, Nancy Werlin — 85
- *Family Rings*, Michele Glorie Palmer — 86
- *Stride Piano*, Alice Clark — 88
- *Warp & Weft*, Joyce O'Donnell Maroney — 90
- *Hairloom*, Rebecca Clever — 91
- *Daughters of Ann*, Anna Marie Nachman — 92
- *Reel Time*, Liz Maroney — 94
- *Layer by Layer*, Nina Snyder — 96
- *Faccia Malute*, Christy Diulus — 98

SECTION SIX — WHO AM I? WHO ARE YOU? 101
- *Growing Up Half Jewish*, Jane I. Cash — 102
- *Good-Woman*, Connie Cousins — 104
- *My Dear Little Girl*, Sally Eckert — 106
- *Pumpkin*, Elizabeth Ashe — 109
- *Recovery*, Marilyn Silverman — 110
- *Sweet, Sturdy, Thrifty, and Original, Caroline*, Douglas James Glorie — 112
- *Wealthy*, Kirti Patel — 114
- *SPS*, Josephine Carubia — 116
- *Grandmother's Balcony*, Sinem Turgut — 118

SECTION SEVEN — LOST AND FOUND 121
- *Irish Whiskey, Neat*, Richard W. Conklin — 122
- *My Mother's Arms*, Ann Seltzer Pangborn — 124
- *Sanctuary on the Sapelo*, Josephine Carubia — 125
- *Reconstructing the Tower of Babel*, Rebecca Miller — 128
- *Second Chance*, Kyung Ryoon Kim — 130
- *Hurricane Bob Salad, August 1991*, Josephine Carubia — 133
- *Une Grande Aventure*, Kate Staley — 134
- *A Valentine Story*, Hattie Mae Coleman Gerhart Johnson — 138
- *Guardian Angel*, Darlene Throckmorton — 140
- *Colored Circles*, Victoria Tilney McDonough — 141
- *Christmas Socks*, John Bellanti — 146

SECTION EIGHT — UNIVERSAL SINGULARITIES 149
- *We Don't Eat Shrimp*, Petya Kirilova-Grady — 150
- *One of a Kind*, Alyce Paquette Moore — 152
- *I Married a Mother, 1991*, Fritz Eckert — 154
- *The Bold One*, Elaine Palmer — 155
- *What Would Aunt Nettie Say?*, Nina Snyder — 158
- *Skating With Mom*, Jane Richards — 160
- *Savings*, Paul W. Bixby — 164
- *Until You Got Here*, Beth McLaughlin — 165
- *Je Suis Mama*, Kimberly Townsend — 166

ABOUT THE CONTRIBUTORS 168

Women ... learn to adapt. I watched my mother do it, and my grandmother too. Through marriage and divorce, through too little money or too much, too many children or too few, through sorrow and joy and all the longings that were not and never could be named, women, I learned, adapted.

At first the lives of women frightened me. They seemed so fragile, so dependent on fathers and husbands and brothers and lovers. Gradually, though, I noticed how supple their lives were beneath the surface. Then I realized it was this flexibility that enabled them to survive. I saw, too, that sooner or later, by choice or by chance, most women faced the task of adapting to a future on their own. When at my most optimistic, I thought of it as independence; in darker moods, as survival. Either way, women had to do it.

Alice Steinbach

Without Reservations: The Travels of an Independent Woman

Introduction

A need to tell and hear stories is essential to the species Homo Sapiens – second in necessity apparently after nourishment and before love and shelter.
                                    Reynolds Price

This book is full of stories and it is a story in itself. It begins more than ten years ago at a time when Michele and I had already lost many significant women in our family and were about to lose yet another. We began to ask people close to us to tell us their stories about mothers, aunts, grandmothers, sisters, and other influential women in their own families. Over the years, our circle expanded to people we didn't know and people from other countries and traditions. We discovered that we were sustained in our losses by the momentum and sweep of the stories we were collecting.

Telling stories is one of the ways we create and sustain our families in every culture. Along the way, we create ourselves too. Some of the stories in this book came to us easily like colorful boats riding high on rivers of laughter and joy. Gathering those stories was like touching the brimming water of an overfilled cup. Other stories were the result of long processes of meandering through the jungles of the past to locate the tangled vines of critical turning points. In a few cases, the very notion of telling a story, of giving away family secrets, was a cause for great anxiety. Some stories were private journeys, shared in confidence. Those stories are fully a part of the experience of the book, even though they are not in the book.

Stories, we found, are everywhere: abundant and ripe, tickling or creepy-crawling just under the skin. Even when someone is quiet and shy, we may imagine a tiny movie screen, about the size of a forehead. It's playing a beach scene from the last century, or a short loop of words quickly wished unsaid, or a thirty-year-old tantrum still occupying a central place in the mind.

The true stories in *About Her* reflect intimate moments and private thoughts as well as war, national holidays, and a great variety of traditions. Some will make you laugh out loud, and some will bring tears to your eyes. We listened to dozens and dozens of stories and collaborated with storytellers to bring you this selection of the most poignant and vivid narratives. We focused this anthology on stories mostly about women, and recognize that this is just one turn of the kaleidoscope of human experience. It is broad enough to include topics of significance like identity, tradition, survival, creativity, mortality, and joy, and yet allows us to offer readers a convergence of themes.

Technically, these life experiences are past and gone; the words in this book are just marks on the page, but good stories create a powerful and mysterious enchantment. They speak directly to the human heart within each of us. We hope you will be touched and inspired as we have been by every unique story in the book. We are tremendously grateful to all of the writers and storytellers who trusted us enough to give us the gift of a story. This includes writers whose stories do not appear in the book for a variety of reasons. We appreciate all of the magnificent stories that were shared with us.

About Her is organized as a tour through different perspectives and attitudes about memory and the past. For example, the perspective of beings measured in inches and months, not feet and years can appear as a foreign country. We big people never really know what impressions we make on children until many years later. Or what scenes they will remember from a chaotic family occasion. Or what they overheard when adults thought they were sleeping. Childhood is a treasure chest of stories.

Journeys come in both literal and metaphorical flavors and families are complex systems with bodies in constant motion. Thus, we have narratives about the rhythms of locomotion where steps may be taken forward, backward, toward, or away, and where any step may be a stumble or as graceful as a ballet. These migrations may reveal more about us than an electrocardiogram or CAT scan.

A photograph is just the briefest slice of a moment in time, but it may open a magical door to storytelling. The drama of life, in all its sensory fullness, comes rushing back through the window of the image, even if a camera was not available to capture the frame.

We have gathered several kinds of "greats" and "grands" under this heading: inspirational and wise elders, magnificent survivors of devastating events, and at least one full-fledged, grand-dame dressed in furs. Here are women of grand gestures, large personality, immense fortitude, and enormous heart.

Women often speak in domestic metaphors, using the objects and activities of making a home to describe other events and experiences. Sewing, cooking, gardening, and child-rearing are all rich with vivid images to express meaning. The bonds of family and the lines of inheritance can be described through fibers, cloth, wallpaper, home-made music, and more. As Carol Shields says, "The connective tissue between us is taut with detail." Thus are we woven into family, knit into relationship, stitched through time, and linked in spirit.

Perhaps the most important question everyone is asking in these stories is about identity. Storytellers are seeking and finding hints about who a mysterious antecedent creature was and who they have become as a result of this influence, OR despite this influence.

Losing someone and being lost are equally extreme experiences, and both apply to actual persons and also to feelings of being disoriented, abandoned, and vulnerable. In some of the stories of *About Her*, storytellers find themselves, along with other valuables once thought lost.

About Her celebrates the unique and exceptional qualities of women in everyday life and in momentous times. In some ways, we are all the same. And yet, each of us is distinctive with rare and irreplaceable qualities, talents, genius, and appeal. Even when this inimitable package is quirky to the point of causing discomfort, we can still smile in retrospect as memory proves how remarkable our singularities are.

This book is a catalog of gemstones; a portfolio of international heritage sites; a museum of artifacts and replicas; a variety show of reality skits; a retrospective of independent documentary films; and a harvest of the heart. Grounded in the five senses, it spins out into a multi-dimensional world of vivid recollection and profound recognition. From baby steps to funeral tears; from Grandma's soup and homemade bread to beach vacations and hospital beds: LIFE is here!

***

So many people inspired and supported us in the process of creating this book and many others contributed to the process of bringing it to completion. Behind the scenes, out of the picture, and alive only in memory are all of the women whose fascinating stories beg to be set down for others to experience. We appreciate all of the friends, family, storytellers, and colleagues who encouraged us and who spread the word to help us invite such a broad spectrum of writers and storytellers.

As we moved from gathering stories to designing and producing a book, Ken Volk was professional to the max and creative *on beyond zebra* to help us realize our vision. Ken Hull shared his own publishing experiences and contacts, and we can only hope to achieve half his success with *Going Local: An Adventurer's Guide to Unique Eats, Cool Pubs & Cozy Cafes of Central Pennsylvania* and its sequel(s). Michael Azevedo contributed just what we needed at the moment we needed it, and the book's title is the result. Vincent Colapietro – patron of the arts, verbal virtuoso, and generous heart – has been a source of motivation and relentless encouragement on this and many other endeavors.

It has been said that the stories we tell about our lives, and even the stories we imagine about other lives, nurture our spirits with necessary consolation. We would add that stories nurture our spirits with necessary joy as well. We thank all of our contributors for sharing both the consolation and the joy.

Josephine Carubia
Michele Glorie Palmer

SECTION ONE

The View of a Child

My childhood had no narrative; it was all just a combination of air and no air: waiting for life to happen, the body to get big, the mind to grow fearless. There were no stories, no ideas, not really, not yet. Just things unearthed from elsewhere and propped up later to help the mind get around. At the time, however, it was liquid, like a song – nothing much. It was just a space with some people in it. ... But one can tell a story anyway.

Lorrie Moore

Heaven Beneath Her Feet

A recollection: On a sun-drenched May afternoon a house is filled with grown-ups whose moods are alternately somber and boisterous and whose clothing seems awfully dark and heavy for the warmth of this spring day. To a seven-year-old boy, itchy in the suit he was tasked to wear to his grandfather's funeral, the incongruities of the scene are dizzying: laughter mixed with tears, solemn utterances marinating amidst the small talk, sloppy wet kisses inflicted by total strangers upon unsuspecting cheeks … and all those cold cuts!

Performing an escape act he would repeat innumerable times throughout his life, the boy slinks toward the first unobstructed door he can find to seek solace on the grass, beneath the trees. Hoping that solitude would yield clarity, he leans against the tree and gazes heavenward only to realize at that moment, he is not alone. The boy's grandmother, the wife of the man just laid to earth, has beaten him to this leafy refuge.

"Looking for something?" she asks. Embarrassed, the boy admits he was wondering if it were possible to see a body (or soul, as the nuns have instructed him) as it makes its way to heaven. "Only at night," my grandmother – my beloved Nana – replies. "That's why there are shooting stars. When it gets dark, we'll look together." And in that instant, Mary Mahoney gifted me yet again – in a moment that should have been about easing her grief – with her unfailing openness, acceptance, and wise simplicity.

We sat together for a while, she being no more eager to head back indoors than I, and marveled at how tall the dogwood trees had grown over the previous years. And somehow we came to talk about the ever unfolding circle of life, without ever using such words. Nana knew nothing of metaphors or allusions, and would likely have felt pretentious spouting them if she did. She reminded me of God always having a plan and how He was tempering our collective loss with the imminent arrival of what would turn out to be my little brother, a mere three days later.

The loss my grandmother endured that day was but one of fate's many unsuccessful attempts to dislodge her unfailingly hopeful and appreciative spirit. Cast from her own family of origin in Cork, Ireland at age seven, she journeyed to America with a loving uncle only be thrust into the role of servant girl by his less-than-loving stateside wife. Resilient to her core, she found for herself a surrogate family down the road, through her friendship with another little girl named Mary. Theirs was a bond that would endure for more than eight decades and resulted in my Nana marrying her friend Mary's brother, the man she buried on that May morning.

There are those among us who appear lit from within: those who, contrary to all situational evidence, beam with a grace and wisdom that comforts and encourages. Nana's light served as a beacon to me on many occasions; she would offer a sly wink as I was being reprimanded by a stressed-out parent or as we chatted aimlessly while strolling the wide and tree-hushed streets around Harvard's Divinity School where she worked in a custodial position.

"Isn't that beautiful?" Nana would often make this comment, more as a statement of faith and belief than a question. To her, beauty was everywhere: in the changing of the seasons, a random gathering of clouds, the cacophony of her grandchildren's laughter, the comforting silence of her kitchen at dawn. Though she passed her days with an open heart and smiling eyes, Nana was nobody's fool. She'd witnessed, firsthand, enough duplicity and disappointment to know that beauty's opposing image could easily prevail and poison one's perspective if allowed. She withstood these assaults on her chosen worldview by pairing her hopeful optimism with a sly and leveling sense of humor. With a handful of choice words, she could puncture the pomposity of the most gaseous windbag (she'd have a field day with me!) without a trace of malice.

Another recollection: Twenty-two years have passed since that warm day in May. I am living in a seventeenth-century farmhouse in Brewster, Massachusetts, filling my days typing cover letters and sending out resumes (in between arduous bike rides to the beach) and occupying my nights waiting tables. My mother, sister, and Nana have come to visit. Early one July morning, I am up just after dawn for my jog to the nearby gym. On my bleary-eyed stumble from bedroom to kitchen, I am frozen in my tracks by a vision: Nana, past eighty, has hauled a lawn chair out to the spacious yard's center and is sitting in reverie, sipping tea while being serenaded by a chorus of mourning doves. I drink in this tableau for some minutes, seeking the lesson to be learned in her perfect stillness. Finally, I open the screen door and slip out quietly to greet her. Without breaking the spell she's conjured for herself, her eyes meet mine and she says, "Heaven. This is just heaven. How could anyone want anything more?"

Her insight was her strength and her legacy. Her joyful optimism buoyed her in mind and body: hit by a car and cracking her pelvis after stepping from a bus one February morning of her eighty-sixth year, she was nonetheless digging deep in the dirt planting flowers that very spring. The doctors called it a minor miracle. Those of us who'd tapped into her sustaining secret knew that where Nana was concerned, it was all miracles.

A final recollection: A man approaching forty settles into the window seat of an eastbound jet for a six-hour flight across the country. In his mind, he travels across the years and pans the river of his memory for those golden nuggets of Nana stories he'll need to shape into the eulogy he'll be giving twenty-four hours hence. He knows already that his meager words will fall well short of capturing the vastness of her spirit, the depth of her delightfulness. As the plane climbs ever higher toward those heavens in which she now resides, a spray of stars begins to pierce the darkness. Did he imagine or really see one particularly bright shooting star across his field of vision? It didn't really matter, for in that moment the logjam of memories loosened and the fitting words poured forth as readily as the tears that fell from his eyes.

Michael Azevedo

Early Morning at Roundfield

We swung and dangled together from the rail and the banister at the top of the staircase sometime before 6:00 a.m. We twisted and fidgeted, trying to peer around the rail of the staircase, trying to get a glimpse of the kitchen to see whether the light was on yet. Did we hear her in there? And did we dare go downstairs? We were aching to see her, this tall, happy German woman with a pixie-ish sense of humor, the woman who had strictly set this time, 6:00 a.m., before which we could absolutely not come down and disturb her quiet breakfast alone. Was it 6:00 a.m. yet? We couldn't tell time, so we were just guessing. We had no way of knowing. I suppose we thought that when we had waited sufficiently and could not wait any longer, then it must be 6:00 a.m.

My grandparents built this staircase, and the house around it, toward the end of the Great Depression, in the late 1930s. The New York estate included twenty-four acres of land, which was in an oval shape. My grandmother, who had aristocratic notions, named it "Roundfield" because, I suppose, "Ovalfield" doesn't sound very good. They built a white colonial house with green shutters and the grand front staircase with wide stairs and a sweeping banister that ended in a large round swirl at the bottom. We always tried to slide down it, with varying results.

Eventually the three or four of us would lose patience and run down the staircase, which could easily fit three children running side by side. We ran through the hall and took a left into the kitchen, where she would be finishing up her breakfast. Strict as she was (she had been a schoolteacher in New York City for forty years and didn't take nonsense from anybody), she was always happy to see us whenever we happened to descend upon her. To this day, I have no idea at what time we besieged her.

I had assumed all these years that she was an early riser by nature. "No," said my mother recently, "she liked to sleep late. She got up early for you children, and for me and Dad." I felt a little foolish that I had never understood this. After forty years of teaching first and second graders all week long, there are plenty who would opt not to get up at that awful hour with their grandchildren. How good of her to give us the gift of her time, and always to be happy, not cranky, with us.

Much later, I used to listen patiently to long stories of her life and travels. After retiring, she and my grandfather had traveled around the world, which had been their lifelong dream. The story that he, an animal lover, had boxed with a kangaroo in Australia, has entertained my family for generations.

After he died, she moved into the house next to my parents. I suppose she was a little lonely, and she loved to talk.

My grandmother and grandfather on the Egyptian leg of their world tour.

As a teenager, sometimes I wanted to leave and do something a little more interesting. But I thought to myself, "No, she's lonely, and it's not polite to leave. Stay and listen until she is done!"

So I stayed, and I listened. It was nice. I found out things I had never known about her. I learned that her father was a cooper by trade and that he built horse-drawn carriages in the early 1900s. He was the first on the block to own an automobile, and my grandmother, who was certainly not a good driver in her later years, learned to drive immediately on that early Ford.

Now, I finally understand that just as I gave her the gift of my time, so she had, many years before, and many times before, given me the gift of hers. I remember it ... so early in the morning ... waiting, dangling, on the great staircase of Roundfield.

Juliet Silveri

The Folder

When Maggie's mom picked her up at the end of her first day of kindergarten, she asked how the day went. "Good," Maggie answered. Then she seemed to reconsider, and started to pout, gradually working herself up into tears. "My teacher is mean. She made me have the pink folder, and the boys got to have the blue." Maggie's mom sighed. "I'm sorry honey, but some people think that way. It doesn't make sense, I know." The next day, when she dropped Maggie off, she saw two boxes of folders, hot pink and bright blue, side by side near the hamster's cage. She asked Mrs. Handler why she'd divided the folders that way. Mrs. Handler made a scrunched-up face that told Maggie's mom she thought a preposterous "political" agenda was in the air. "Oh, that, it's just for convenience." She waved her hand dismissively in the direction of the boxes; it was clear she had no interest in changing her system.

It wasn't long before the notes started coming home, escalating in their frustration. "Maggie needs to learn to use her time more wisely." "Maggie just isn't listening well." "Maggie can't keep her hands and feet to herself." "Maggie got out of line and went to the bathroom without asking!" At the parent-teacher conference, Mrs. Handler said that Maggie was making "bad choices" in her friends. "Why don't you encourage her to be friends with Melissa or Veronica," she suggested, naming two particularly docile little girls. Maggie's mom had noticed how Mrs. Handler often placed her hands affectionately on the shoulders of such girls while talking to their parents on family night. The girls would blush with pleasure, peeking at their parents from behind their bangs, feeling safe and chosen.

Once, Mrs. Handler, in a deliberate show of warmth, had tried the hands-on-shoulders posture with Maggie, who squirmed away. The teacher pretended not to notice, but an especially furious, picky note came home the next day. "I'm losing my patience with Maggie; I wouldn't let her hand in her work late, and later I found it on the floor!" Maggie claimed the work had dropped out of her Thomas-the-Train backpack, which had numerous zippers that she sometimes forgot to close. But Mrs. Handler was convinced that Maggie had thrown the work to the floor on purpose, in a fit of rebellious anger. She punished Maggie by not allowing her to read out loud that day. "I was at the top!" Maggie sobbed to her mother, referring to the kindergarten reading program, which permitted them to advance only one book at a time, "And now Bryce and Veronica are both ahead of me, and I'll never be able to catch up!"

Maggie's best friend was Caleb, a fearless little boy who matched Maggie in energy and exuberance. They had been in the same preschool class, where the teacher was more tolerant of their loud laughter and sudden, breakaway runs from circle-time. "Me and Caleb, we like to be wild together!" Maggie told her mom.

Many people at the kindergarten thought Maggie and Caleb looked alike. They had the same light brown skin, the same round, baby faces; they both wore cornrows, and were close in height. The white teachers confessed to Maggie's mom, with embarrassment, that they sometimes thought Maggie was Caleb and vice versa. But Maggie didn't mind, not at all. She liked being confused with Caleb, just as she liked dressing up in a suit and tie, matching her dad's, when they went to a fancy restaurant. She had an underwear drawer full of jockey briefs – the real thing with the front opening. When strangers on the street called her "little fellow" and "buddy," she poked her mother in the ribs and whispered "Don't tell!"

Caleb, however, was not so happy being mistaken for a girl. When he showed up one day with barely a half-inch of fuzzy stubble, Maggie came home in a state. "Why can't I have my hair like Caleb's?" she whined over and over. Her mom searched her mental file of replies to questions such as this, and couldn't find a very good one. "Why don't you wait until you're a little older, and then decide?" Maggie's mom suggested to Maggie, ashamed of her own cowardice and feeling vaguely traitorous to her daughter. "I'll still feel the same way then," Maggie said with conviction, then raced away on her Heelys.

The last day of the term, Maggie brought all her kindergarten stuff home: pictures of (what appeared to be) Thanksgiving turkeys, the leaf collages, the crumbling remains of various "science experiments" with unidentifiable substances. And the hot pink folder with all the little "essays" that they had written during the term. From the outside, the folder looked just as it had, lying in the box in class. But when Maggie's mom opened it up, she saw that the inside had been recolored, in chaotic but purposeful circles and slashes, a deep, deep blue. On the top of the pile of papers was a page containing nothing but Maggie's, name, ascending in size:

Maggie. Maggie. Maggie. Maggie. Maggie. Maggie. Maggie.

Susan Bordo

Author's note: "The Folder" is a true story, although names have been changed.

Saved by an Angel

My mother, Alfonzina Carubia, was born in Cianciana, Sicily and moved to America at a very young age. My father, Ernest D'Ambrosio, was born in Castelluccio, Italy and also moved to America at a very young age. My father was thirty-seven years old when I was born, and my mother was twenty-eight. I was their favorite son for thirteen months until my brother Andrew was born. Six years later my brother Ernest was born. We lived on a farm in Milton, New York.

Life on the farm was difficult at times, but we had lots of cousins to play with, got to eat the cookie batter from the bowl, always had spaghetti on Sunday, and our outhouse had two seats. Mother watched over all of us like a loving guardian angel, mending our wounds, protecting us from the cold winters and rescuing us from angry roosters.

The most memorable experience when Mother came to my rescue took place when I was seven years old. I loved listening to the Lone Ranger on the radio. When we got a TV, cowboy shows were my favorites, including not only the Lone Ranger but also Roy Rogers and Gene Autry. They would sometimes show off their skills with a rope, twirling and roping things. When I got old enough to pick up a rope, I would practice twirling and roping things, too.

Our front yard was located along Milton Turnpike, and not too many cars would come by. Those who did were usually neighbors. One day, I was in the front yard practicing with a rope and I heard a car coming down the hill. I decided that I had roped just about everything in the yard and that a car would make a good notch on my rope. So I roped that car and it came to a screeching halt. I, however, did not. I ran for my life.

When I threw the rope, I never thought I would actually lasso the car. It is a good thing that I was not attached to the rope or I would not be writing this story. Since I did not have a horse upon which to make my escape, I headed for the hills (upstairs) on foot.

There were few hiding places in this territory, so I had to choose quickly and well. I ended up in my parents' room, under the bed. I picked this hideout because of its strategic advantages. I was a little guy and the bed was big. As I settled into my defensive position (under the middle of the bed), I could hear my father and the driver of the car talking. When the talking stopped, the footsteps got louder and louder as they came up the stairs. I was sure a large posse was on my trail. When I was finally spotted and cornered, my father tried to get his hands on me, but every time he would reach for me or move the bed, I would move with the bed. He even lifted the bed off the floor but discovered he could not grab me while holding the bed up. He got his belt out and tried to get me with that, but with each move he made, I made a counter move. I compare this strategic defense with that of the Spartans at the Thermopolis pass. This went on for some time until an angel came to my rescue.

In her soft voice, my mother calmed my father. I finally came out of hiding and into her arms as my father watched helplessly. I think he was waiting to see if he could somehow get his hands on me, but he loved her, too, and was unable to breach her sanctuary. Anyway, I was sparred a lynching (severe beating), which I probably deserved. My mother saved me for a future of more adventures. Even though she had calmed my dad, I stayed very close to her for the rest of the day to make sure I would not be ambushed. Her influence on our family still guides me and those who knew her. She was truly a living angel.

Joseph (l.) and his brother Andrew rescued once again by their mother.

Joseph D'Ambrosio

A Twelve-year-old Girl

She cried and cried, alone on the quiet road from her mother's home to a nearby lake. Many questions appeared in her mind. She could not understand why her mother was so close to that man; why now she was more frequently angry or shouted at her.

What were the mistakes she had committed? She had come home from school one hour later than normal. Could that be the reason? She had bought small fish that were not fresh and that her mother did not like. Could that be the reason?

The twelve-year-old girl hurt everywhere, but most of all, she hurt in her heart. Could she – an above-average student in a gifted class – be compared with an animal in terms of intelligence? Her heart was broken.

Her mother had been the person she loved most in the world. Her mother had promised to take care of her after the divorce and not marry again. Her mother had suspected that her father would remarry.

The girl could not believe that the current situation was real. She wondered if there was anyone who loved and cared for her. She just wanted to go straight to the lake and sink.

She imagined the feeling of sinking down until cold water occupied her body and she could not breathe anymore. That would not be a painful feeling. She kept walking toward the lake, thinking that because she could not swim, she would certainly die if she jumped into the lake. Many children had died there while swimming.

If she died, people would talk tomorrow about a twelve-year-old student who committed suicide, and they would be curious to find the reason for the suicide.

Thinking about her father reminded her of his words: "I'll always be there for you and I will always want you to live with me." She burst into tears again, turned away from the lake, and ran straight to her father's home. From that day on, she lived with her father and her seventy-five-year-old grandmother.

The girl's grandmom used to be an active person. Every day, she cooked for the family and sometimes she taught the girl how to prepare meals so she could become a good wife in the future.

One day, when the girl got home from school at 5:00 p.m., the house was dark. It was winter and the electricity had gone off. She called her grandmother, and she could barely hear a low and weak voice. Her grandmother was lying on the kitchen floor. Grandmom whispered that she fell while she was cooking, and she could not move. She was in pain all over her body.

The twelve-year-old girl was really scared and worried about what would happen to her grandmom. From that day on, Grandmom was paralyzed on half of her body, but she still lived at home with the girl and her father. Now, the family had one more member, a housekeeper.

Every week, the girl's dad gave her money to buy groceries for the family. Every morning, she woke up at 6:00 a.m. and ran to the local market to buy fresh groceries. She brought breakfast and groceries back home by 6:30 a.m. Before going to school, she always remembered to tell the housekeeper to feed Grandmom breakfast and what food to prepare for lunch.

Sometimes, the girl could not wake up on time, and she was late for school. Each late time counted one mistake in the book of conduct for a group of ten or twelve students in the class. If a student had a certain number of mistakes in this book, the student's conduct could be classified as bad and he or she would not be awarded "Excellent Student" at the end of the semester even though the student's GPA was overqualified. She was always afraid of that.

Fortunately, the girl had a guardian angel who was also her aunt. The aunt was a very busy person with a husband, two daughters, a job teaching school, a live-in mother-in-law, and many friends who relied upon her. Still, she found time to be like a second mother to the girl, buying her school clothes every year, giving her spending money, and taking care of her when she was sick.

The aunt gave the girl a million times more than just new clothes and money. She gave her wisdom as well. When the twelve-year-old girl grew older and had her first boyfriend, this aunt really took action. She asked a lot of questions about his family and his education. She was not satisfied with this young man, and said that the girl deserved to be with someone better. She gave many examples of women who lived their lives unhappily because the wife is progression-oriented while the husband is not. Finally, the girl began to agree with her, and broke up with this boyfriend.

If it was not for her aunt's encouragement and actions, the girl would not have had the strength to leave this relationship. Without this help, she would not have had the chance to meet the wonderful man who would become her husband.

When the girl married, her aunt told her how to be a good wife and how to treat her husband's family. When it comes time to be a mother, this fortunate girl has a wonderful role model to follow.

Hoasua (Vietnam)

Gramma and Barbie

"Gramma, wanna play Barbies?" It was the typical question for the typical five year-old. My world of Barbies was my world of happiness, and to share it with Gramma was even better.

"Sure, Sweetie Pie," she would reply every time. I would drag out my box of Barbies, then return to the playroom for the box of clothes. It was our normal routine and it had been forever.

As the years passed, I was somewhere between wanting to become a teenager and desiring to remain a kid forever. I wanted to grow up more than anything, but I didn't want to leave my Barbie world behind. None of the cool middle-schoolers played with Barbies anymore. Barbies had gone out with a vengeance and now makeup was what all the cool girls spent their time with. Yet, every time I went to Gramma's house, it was okay to play Barbies. And, that's just what we did.

When I was eleven or twelve, I was still young enough to need to go somewhere when I stayed home from school and my parents had to work. It was convenient to drop me off at Gramma's house. That's where I was happy, and my parents need not worry about me. Once I got there, Gramma and I would watch the morning talk shows; then the Barbies would come out.

All of my Barbies were older. I had none of the neat, modern Barbies that came out because I didn't have spending money and even if I did, I wouldn't be caught dead in the Barbie aisle of the local toy store. Barbies were the last thing I needed to think about when I wanted to improve my cool, junior-high status. So, Gramma and I would use the time I spent at her house to go through the WalMart flyer and circle the Barbies that I would like to have. Gramma would take care of the shopping, and by the time the holidays came around, it was assured that I would go home with at least two or three new, fun Barbies.

Gramma and I had so much fun with Barbies. When we played, I was in a fantasy world with not a single care in my mind. The only thing I had to worry about was whether Gramma would remember the difference between Barbie and Skipper. And, when she forgot, I would remind her, "Gramma, Barbie is the oldest; Skipper is her younger sister." And Gramma would play along every time.

It's funny how life turns out. It was a fact that I loved Barbies, and it was quite clear that Gramma loved to play with me. When I got a bit older, the passion that I shared with Gramma for Barbies wore out. It's ironic that when Gramma died, my love for Barbies suddenly did too.

Taryn Snyder

Taryn's grandmother, Catherine "Kay" Snyder, at age five or six with one of her dolls.

Life and Death

I never knew that my aunt was dying. She had been crippled with rheumatoid arthritis for all of my life and I was used to seeing her in a wheelchair. I remember her bed in the living room of the house she shared with my grandmother. Her potty chair was hidden behind a screen.

It was hard for my mother to explain why my aunt was sick. In my family an aspirin was considered powerful medicine and illness was the result of weakness. I knew that we were strong because my grandmother had raised three daughters by herself. Her husband had been killed by a train on his way home from the produce market when my mother was still in diapers.

My aunt had overdone it in college, my mother finally told me. She had loved nice things and had worked too hard, burned the candle at both ends, held too many jobs, hadn't gotten enough rest. "Remember always to take care of yourself, Anne, and get enough sleep," my mother would say over and over again. Weakness was always a step away.

My grandmother looked stern to me. She had been widowed so suddenly with three young daughters and the crops to harvest for winter. What did she think about during those long nights on the farm? In the picture album I see the young mother standing proudly next to her husband. She is smiling. "One of the finest young men of the vicinity is gone. He was progressive and industrious, a lover of mankind in general, and well worth knowing and having as a friend," said the newspaper account of the terrible accident and his death.

The smile I remember most was my Aunt Margaret's. She loved me and I loved her. It was as simple as that. I never noticed her crippled hands or her bloated face. I would tell her about my life, and when I ran out of things to say, I would make up stories just to see her smile. She must have been in tremendous pain. I never knew it.

She trained her cocker spaniel to pick up the mail when it came through the front door slot and bring it to her. I watched in awe. She ran a little bakery from her kitchen and used her home economics degree to bake cherry pies with lattice-crust tops and beautiful, huge, fragrant loaves of bread. She taught me how to bake, sew, knit, and purl. We had elegant picnics together on a card table in the back yard. How could I have missed noticing those twisted hands holding the knitting needles so patiently for me?

Aunt Margaret went to a sanitarium for experimental treatments with a new drug called cortisone. Who knew what miracle might happen? When she came home, she always had a bit of sherry in a crystal glass before she went to bed. My grandmother, a Christian temperance woman, would take a glass of sherry, too. Did they figure that such small sins didn't matter for those who already knew what Hell was?

Suddenly, my aunt was confined to her bed and then went to the hospital. Mercifully, it didn't take her too long to die. My mother was so deeply shocked by the experience that she told me how the nurses would hold their noses as they passed by my aunt's rotting body. I was fourteen and knew nothing of death. Her funeral was a blur of relatives and their hats. My father and brother were there, but they drove home afterward while my mother, my aunt Mary Gertrude, my grandmother, and I went back to the quiet house. I remember coming awake in a bed in the upstairs bedroom with cool sheets against my face and a familiar doggy smell. I could hear my mother and grandmother talking softy in the room below. I heard my name.

"Anne ... I guess Margaret wanted everything to go to Anne. Her sewing machine, her set of silver ... "

The list was short, but each thing was completely my aunt, her skill, her love of beautiful things. Then one of them said, "Anne doesn't seem very upset."

"She hasn't cried," said my mother's voice. "I guess she's too young."

In the upstairs bedroom, I was speechless with my grief. No comforting stories of my Aunt Margaret in Heaven were spun for me. We were strong. We didn't talk about it. I rolled over and went to sleep.

Anne Allan Whitney

Marks of Our Labors

My homework on one side
And her flour on the other.

My mother rolls dough
As I write answers.

Turning her back to me,
Bending to open the oven,
My giggles parade through the space.

On the back of her blue pants
Are long white handprints
Where she wiped the flour off her hands.

Marks of her labor
Like ink on my fingers.

She asks why I laugh
And I call Dad for a picture.

Shel Julian Kessel

SECTION TWO

Life's Journeys

We shall not cease from exploration, and the end of all our exploring will be to arrive where we started and know the place for the first time.

T. S. Eliot

Driving to the Beach

My mother and I have a loving, tortured relationship. Anyone watching us would discern our usual pattern quickly enough: affirm our mutual love affectionately, then proceed to drive each other nuts. Absolutely nuts. As if under the spell of some gravitational pull that draws us inexorably together, at times we seem fated solely to push each other's buttons. Some say that defines "soulmate."

A talented psychic once said my mother and I were sisters who served as nurses during the first World War. Then she said something about forgiveness, and tears began to well up from deep within. After 104 years of life (ages thirty-eight and sixty-six combined) and how many of therapy, Mom and I have come to accept each other as more or less independent beings with love, respect, and forgiveness. We still drive each other crazy sometimes – I guess it's the way of life – but less frequently now.

In fact, we have rediscovered something, a kind of no-fly zone: the car. A few years ago, a shift in our dispersed family layout changed the logistics of our annual summer treks to the beach near New Bedford, Massachusetts. As a result, Mom generously offered to pick me up enroute at the train station in Providence, Rhode Island. So began our extended road-trip sessions.

Building on the tradition her father enforced of no arguments over dinner, my mother has always stipulated there is to be no arguing in the car. Driving, of course, puts more than the mere smooth digestion of a pleasant meal at stake; given the vitriol that can erupt between us, our lives quite simply depend on détente behind the wheel. So, relieved from our roles as relentlessly loving antagonists, in the car we find ourselves bound together in a common goal: getting to the beach alive depends on forty-five minutes of amiable conversation. Compliant but wary, we sheath our weapons and cease fire.

For summer upon languid summer, I have sought regular refuge at my family's summer cottage by the beach. A quaint little spot, it lies nestled in a rural farming town no one has ever heard of, lost on the shore between New Bedford and Providence. I always look forward to the annual ritual of the train ride north. Offering a transition from my harried, single, New York City working-woman persona to a slower paced, more human, if more textured, sojourner, the rides are filled with window gazing, time drifting, life musings, taking stock.

By the time I arrive in Providence, I have had plenty of time to prepare for this moment when I am once again a daughter. I see my loving mother, ever smiling and hopeful, delighted to be greeting me, her only girl. I can feel her version of love radiating toward me, though it comes on anxious, needy tentacles. Despite my softened state, I am stiffening again, but keep walking toward her.

Resistance is now climbing up the center of my back as my shoulders start to hunch, bracing for the onslaught of questions cum monologue that is about to ensue. "Are you okay, Dear? Is everything alright? How was the train trip? How is that sprained ankle doing? Is it going to be okay? You know Mrs. Stang had a nasty sprain last week, and you should have seen how black and blue it was." It would maybe be okay if there were pauses for one to answer, but there never seems to be an opening. No space to breathe; no space for me.

I begin to bridle, yet hold my tongue. I have been here before; this time I'll break the pattern and let go. Just ... let go.

I mumble a few pleasantries and give her a warm hug, which she eagerly accepts. Despite the arthritis hobbling her knees, she insists on helping me with my bags. I hand her a light one; we walk to the car. It is understood between us that she will be a passenger for this leg of the journey. I engage the clutch. We drive.

We thread our way through the chronic, jumbled construction detours of downtown Providence. Despite her history as a manic depressive, Mom is pretty solid under intellectual pressure. She rallies to the task of navigating with the focus of a surgeon (the unfulfilled calling of her life, she always said, before the illness sabotaged her). As I clear the on-ramp and merge with Massachusetts drivers on a hot, dusty, notoriously serpentine roller-derby section of the highway, Mom calmly points out when it's time to jockey to a different lane to avoid being swept away in a surprise off-ramp. She knows this road like the back of her hand. Coping with the glaring afternoon sun, I gratefully acknowledge the tip. As the traffic eases, we each sigh and relax slightly. Now the conversation begins. Can we do it?

Strangely, I find that my mother can go on about any subject while we are in the car, and it doesn't bother me. Subjects that would normally drive me to fits of distraction if I felt held captive at the breakfast table now wash over me like a warm bath. In an almost darling way, Mom prates on about the neighbors' new dog, the begonias blooming in her garden, what Mrs. Nelson said at the church supper last week, and sundry other bits of small-town gossip about people I am sure I have never met or only vaguely remember. As I settle behind the wheel, my shoulders begin to release.

As an adult, sitting quietly in the car long enough to truly hear, I have finally begun to understand my mother's way of relating, of expressing her needs. Even twenty years after her divorce, I know it is still hard for her to be alone. I have often wished that I could do more, with long hours of listening as a friend would do, to reassure her of her self-worth despite the tragedies in her life, but the recesses of unmet childhood needs run so deep in us both, indeed stretching back generations, it is difficult to find the strength. Understanding that, accepting it, and learning to keep the space I need for myself has taken some time. Being the female child of this woman has not been easy. I can only hope, if I have a daughter someday, that maybe it will be a little easier for her.

But this ride is okay. No captive, I am driving, adventuring, both in control of and surrendered to my destiny. It is summer and I am free, a "voyageuse sans baggages," a sidewalk-bound New Yorker soon to be a stranger wandering along an endless beach. In this heaven, I am glad to have Mom as my co-pilot, regaling me with the most important minutiae, the intensity of the details at the corners of her life. Ever so slightly detached, it is my pleasure to listen.

She's my mom. Tortured or otherwise, I will always love her, both for who she courageously is, and for the unconditional, if nerve-wracking love she has always given me. Most of all, I will always treasure these rare moments of peace as we grow together, wending our way, these precious moments driving to the beach.

Claire Aldrich

On the Road

It was a truth, universally acknowledged, that my mother, Anne Pinto, had no sense of direction. On driving home from an evening meeting at her church, she zigged when she should have zagged and wound up on a deserted country road in the semi-rural town. Surrounded by cows, she later testified that those bovines had murder in their eyes and that she, a sensible woman, was not going to get out of her car to do battle. So, there she sat, honking her horn and shouting invective. When the cows' curiosity was sated, they ambled off and she found her way home. Dad was beginning to get worried, but knowing her relationship to the points of the compass, he had deferred notifying the search parties.

The mere matter of getting lost never stopped her. She was made for the open highway. Learning to drive as a teenager in 1926 on one of her father's trucks, she hit the road and traveled all of her life. Alaska, the Holy Land, Europe, and Canada were some of her jaunts. At eighty she cruised the Amazon and led the land parties that disembarked to survey the banks of the river. Always outgoing, she could spot someone with a grasp of north and south and thus ensured that she would have a navigator on her rambles. Her own children came early to an understanding of maps in order to defend themselves against interminable car rides.

But of all her many trips, some of the most hilarious were those to the Connecticut shore. Never one to hoard the fun, she always had a gang with her – sisters, nieces, nephews, and friends. Other than her own children, her most constant co-pilot was her mother, Concetta Peters. These expeditions involved less than reliable cars which insured that the trip would include at least one breakdown. Grandma would stand sentry as the rest of us scurried around in search of aid. When the hapless good Samaritan hove into sight, Ma would go into charm mode and we would soon be on the road again.

When I was a child, the trip to the shore took two hours or more (depending on vicissitudes), but, in my mother's youth, the expedition was an all-day affair complete with breakdowns and a big picnic lunch. Gramp got a Model T about 1920. He was shown how to drive by the salesmen where he bought her – driver's licenses didn't exist – but no one bothered to tell him about reverse. So each morning all of the kids piled out of the house and pushed the car out of the barn for Gramp to fire her up and drive off to work. Having mastered that first car, he graduated to a big touring model in order to fit the whole family and assorted friends.

On one trip over the Avon Mountain, the car began to smoke at the peak. Grinding to a halt, Gramp got out to reconnoiter. The kids assisted with a rock under the wheel to act as a brake and Grandma took up guard. When Gramp was finally satisfied that all was well, he called for removal of the rock and started down the mountain. Unfortunately, he left Grandma at the summit and the sibs were in such a state of hilarity that he wasn't informed until well down the road. The story entered family lore, but Grandma never got left behind again.

At first the family camped at the shore. Each person had a cot, and one fine night a skunk decided to have a kip under Florence's bed. The rest of the family went into suspended animation until the guest departed. Soon after, Gramp's thoughts turned to renting a cottage. My mother never forgot the first Sound View homestead with a wrap-around veranda covered with a honeysuckle vine. I never stayed there, but I smell the honeysuckle yet from the power of her description. Many cottages followed. Some rented by Gramp, and later, some by my mother and dad. But they all had this in common: large family gatherings, wonderful food, and almost enough time for swimming and beach exploring.

L to R: Florence Peters, Millie Peters, Lena Malone, and Anne Peters (Pinto) at ages sixteen to twenty.

It remains wonderful to me that my mother executed all of these beach parties, since she actually did not enjoy the shore. But she knew that her children had a passion for it and hence off we went. My Uncle Ed's cottage marked the point where the Connecticut River joined Long Island Sound at the inner lighthouse. Uncle Ed, a World War I veteran, had served on the SS Pocahontas and was ever after a lover of the sea. His cottage was built like a boat and each room had a plaque indicating its function – galley, First Mate, Salon, and, of course, the engine room, a.k.a., the bath. Time there was among the quintessence of the beach days.

When I think back to my childhood, the best times are the gatherings of the clan. My mother was the eldest and took her role as organizer very seriously. After my grandmother's death, Gramp came to live with us and my mother assumed the role of matriarch. The two big events were Christmas Eve, with its Italian tradition of a meal of at least seven types of seafood, and Easter brunch replete with Easter Pizza. Actually a meat pie, the pizza had a filling of ham, hard cooked eggs, and cheese encased in savory egg dough. Fifty pounds of flour, twelve-dozen eggs, and a pound of fresh yeast were the starters.

We had all taken part in the making of the pizzas during my grandmother's life. Little ones fetched things. Bigger people took up stations at either side of the board stretched between two chairs on which stood the huge pan holding the flour mixture. Under Grandma's watchful eye, the dough was flipped over and passed from side to side until the texture was right. The next day, the rolling, filling, and baking of thirty or forty pizzas occurred. The work involved all of my grandmother's daughters and several of the grandchildren. This task passed to my mother who assured her father that it was no problem and she would certainly produce the Easter Pizza that first year without Grandma.

Unfortunately there was no recipe, so Ma just carried on. The dough was finally set and she dropped into bed exhausted. At midnight, my brother John woke her to tell her that the dough was cresting the pan and heading downhill. She told him to punch it down and go to bed. The next morning she opened the basement door to find that the dough had gone over the pan, down the side of the freezer, across the floor and was working on the second step of the staircase. Like its maker, that pizza was made for the open road. This calamity became one of my mother's favorite stories and she dined out on it frequently. She eventually worked out proper proportions for the recipe which I now make each year – with seven pounds of flour.

Nothing stopped her. Neither a broken hip nor a run-away pizza could deter her determination to keep exploring the world around her, to find new places to visit and new experiences to conquer. The open road was always beckoning with unknown delights ahead. As I look back to the kingdom of childhood, it is her gift of the promise of open space that I remember best. And that promise was most tangible to us where the land meets the sea during those long summer evenings.

The adults are all in their beach chairs at the margin of the land. Content after the long picnic, they sit there talking quietly and watching the children who are still clinging to the last light of the day and paddling in the breaking waves. Knowing that the grownups are behind them on guard, the children run with the wind and turn their faces to the freedom and space of the open sea.

Andrea Pinto Lebowitz

A Baseball Story

Innumerable stories have been written about encounters with former Major League baseball players. This may come off as just another one of those. But as I look at the picture sitting on the desk in my office, I can't help but think that this story is different ... made more important, maybe, because time is running out, and I have unfinished business that won't wait much longer.

This story dates back to a time when girls did not play baseball; pre-Title IX. Two generations of girls have been born since then; playing sports with all the advantages that I never had. This story is not about that ... not really. It's about a memory, and a story that I have tried to tell several times to the man involved, but each time words fail me.

Baseball has been in my blood as long as I can remember. My grandmother Sadie, a passionate Red Sox fan, passed the love of the game on to me. From the early 1960s, I have only brief snapshots of memories; Gramma, pitching the ball to me in the back yard. Five years old, skinny and shirtless, I swing with all my might, yelling "Strike!" when I make contact. I guess I confused baseball with bowling back then, and a different grandmother might have let it go. But to her, it was important that I understand the game, and she explained that a strike was good in bowling, but in baseball, it meant something very different.

Another snapshot: watching the Red Sox on a black and white TV, circa 1960, and the man with the funny name is pitching: *Mom-boo-cat*. Although the picture on the TV is grainy, I have a clear memory of my grandmother saying that *Mom-boo-cat* was a great pitcher. Now, I'm sure my grandmother spoke of Ted Williams; she may also have mentioned Earl Wilson and Frank Malzone. But to my five-year-old ears, those were ordinary names. Bill Monbouquette is the name I would remember.

Gramma died in 1988, at the age of ninety-nine after a stroke and a broken hip. But she left a legacy of passion for the game of baseball, passed down to her daughter, her granddaughter, and her great-granddaughter, which brings me to the reason for this story.

In 1996, I celebrated my fortieth birthday with the ultimate fantasy for a Red Sox fan. One of only three women to attend Sports Adventures Red Sox Fantasy Camp in Fort Myers, Florida, I was able to play baseball for a week with those who loved the game as I did. Gramma's girl finally fulfilled her dream of playing for the Boston Red Sox! The bonus, of course, was getting to meet ex-Red Sox players ... famous ones ... like Carl Yastrzemski, George Scott, and Rico Petrocelli. But the man I most wanted to meet was the man with the funny name ... Bill Monbouquette. I wanted to explain to him what meeting him meant to me, and what great memories his name invoked, but I feared that saying "You were my grandmother's favorite player" would sound trivial. I didn't want to insult the man by making him feel old, and secondly, I truly didn't know if he indeed was her favorite player. But his is the name I remember her saying, and I can hear her saying it today as clearly as I heard it when I was five years-old. The real reason for my reluctance is that I feared telling him would cause my throat to close up, and then tears would come. This, of course, was even before Tom Hanks said "There's no crying in baseball." Even so, I never told him, but always thought: "If only Gramma could see me now!"

Over the years, I've returned again and again to Fantasy Camp, and have gotten to know Bill and his wonderful wife Josephine. And, I have had other opportunities to tell him about how important that is, yet words have failed me each time. This year, things are different. Bill Monbouquette has cancer. We weren't sure he would be able to come to camp, but he did. One night after dinner, he walked to the podium to a standing ovation, and told us about his diagnosis, the treatments, and the kindness of the Boston Red Sox and the people at Dana Farber. His throat closed up, and the tears came, and I knew then that sometimes crying in baseball is justified, especially when life has handed out a huge dose of bad luck.

But, back to the picture on my desk, the one I cherish above all others. It is not of Bill and me, but of Bill and my twenty-eight-year-old daughter Jen, taken this year at Fantasy Camp. Despite chemotherapy, he still is looking strong in his gray, Red Sox away uniform; she in her Red Sox home uniform and wearing her catcher's gear. She is looking up at him with great intent while he talks to her. I would like to think they were talking about baseball, but in all likelihood, he

Bill Monbouquette and Courcy's daughter, Jen.

is talking to Jen, a veteran herself, about his pride in his own two sons, both serving our country. The subject doesn't matter. What does matter is that Gramma is looking down, seeing her granddaughter and great-granddaughter playing baseball with the Boston Red Sox, and they have become friends with the man with the funny name, Bill *Mom-boo-cat*. I know she's proud. It's time to tell him how important that is.

Lisa L. Courcy

Dove

Shaune whipped out the zoom lens tonight to get a close-up of a pregnant mama robin. I've been trying to get Deaglan to notice the different birds that come into our yard. It paid off because he squealed with recognition when he saw her land on our deck.

There were also some doves in our small garden snacking on something – Shaune hopes it is not his not his garlic shoots which have started to make an appearance.

The scene made me think about my birth mother. Her name was Cobu. I don't remember her face all that well – it's been just over thirty years since I last saw her. It was the night that my older sister and I had our very first ride in a car.

By that time, Cobu had been living in the streets with our two baby sisters, surviving by cooking meals for people in exchange for scraps of food to feed her babies. Our father had kicked her out of the little mud hut telling her she had to take the babies and leave us two older girls with him to help out. She had allegedly been unfaithful to him. That's what he told all of the neighbors. That's what I believed for a long time.

Our family was extremely poor; my father pulled a rickshaw for a living, and we were Muslim. After she left, we rarely saw our mother. I remember feeling angry at her for not coming back. I was so young. A few times, one of her brothers would come take us to her when our father wasn't around. I remember pleading with her to come home or at least take us with her. It must have been so hard for her to hear us cry.

Then one day she had us brought to her again. This time she took us to a place where a Canadian woman fed us. This woman was either a missionary or a social worker and she told my mother that there was a place she could take my sister and me, a place where we would be clothed and fed and be safe. My mother knew that we had not been eating; she knew that we had been begging on the streets, and she knew that she had to do something. I don't think it happened that first day, but soon after we were again brought to that place. This time we were bathed and given clothes. There are so many details about this that I remember because the experience was so fresh and different from what we had been living ... and it was the last time I ever saw Cobu.

My sister and I were taken to an orphanage in Dhaka (a two-day boat ride away). We never saw or heard from our mother again. Within several months we were adopted and flown to Canada.

I never appreciated Cobu's experience so much as when I had my own child. It's clear to me now that the reason our father exiled her from our home was because she kept giving birth to daughters. He put on her the shame that it brought to him by telling everyone, including us, that she was unfaithful. I can't imagine the courage it took to find a way to save our lives, to give us up because only this would give us a better life than the one we were living.

When I saw the pregnant mama robin and the snacking doves tonight, I thought about Cobu. I thought about her while I fed my baby, while I read him a story, and while I bathed him and rocked him to sleep. I thought about how her name Cobu means dove in Bengali.

Kim McNamara

Priorities

My mom's story is one of self motivation, devotion, and perseverance.

We are a family from the Dominican Republic which is considered a third-world country. My mom was born February 27, 1938 in a poor family and a somewhat dysfunctional household. My grandmother was of Spanish descent with blond hair and blue eyes. My grandfather was a native Dominican with dark skin and light eyes. He never held a steady job and he was not much of a provider. He traveled throughout the country working as a salesman. My grandmother was a stay-at-home mom, who would sew, cook, and bake to provide for her kids. Despite their poor economic situation and because of their strong Catholic beliefs, they had nine children; five girls and four boys.

Getting an education in those days was not a priority. There were two school sessions, one in the morning and another in the afternoon. The children had to share their clothing and their shoes to attend school. The kids who went to the morning session had to rush home to give their siblings the uniforms and shoes so they could go to school in the afternoon. Most of them did not even finish elementary school as children, and never went back after they grew up. They had to find jobs at a very young age to help support the family.

My mom was the exception, because unlike the others, she really did want to finish and get an education. She finished elementary school, but because of the distance and new responsibilities at home with the younger children, she was not able to continue. She married my dad at a very young age. She was sixteen, and my dad was six years older. My mom had her first child (a boy) at the age of seventeen. He was born with Sturge-Weber syndrome. Like her mother before her, my mother also had a big family. We're nine siblings; six boys and three girls, including a set of fraternal twins, my sister and me. Needless to say, she was a full-time, stay-at-home mother and wife.

My second-oldest brother, Ruben, witnessed many years of my mother's struggles with Dad's "machismo" attitudes and unfair treatment. As he grew up and became a young adult, he persisted in telling our mother that someday she would finish her education so she would be able to do better for herself and leave my dad. This seemed very far from becoming a reality for my mom because of her responsibilities with eight children at home by the time she was twenty-nine.

When Ruben was starting ninth grade at thirteen years old, he enrolled himself and our mother in high school. He came home that day and told her to get her uniforms because she was attending school with him. My dad had issues with this decision, but he had no choice but to accept it.

Mom started attending school with all of us when she was thirty-one years old. She had the same school responsibilities as any high-school student. She and my brother used to sit down and do their homework together and help each other every night. Eventually, they both graduated with honors from high school and went on to get a college education. My brother enrolled in the university and earned his degree in civil engineering and my mom became a special education teacher.

When she graduated, she was hired by the local school, and she became the teacher for my oldest brother and the other kids with disabilities. In 1977, Mom had her last child, my brother Leo. Three years later she left my dad, and we all moved to Miami, Florida.

I am happy to say that my mother still lives in Miami and she is now retired and living a healthy and happy life. Who knows where the necessary boost will come from to change a life forever? In some cases, parents give this boost to their children. In our family, it was a child who refused to leave his mother behind.

Miguelina (Millie) Santana

Too Independent

"You're too independent!" exclaimed the Indian uncles and aunties. They meant it in the pejorative sense of the word. It was acceptable when I graduated valedictorian and then went to a top college, but unacceptable when I did things my way. My way often clashed with the Indian way. In my latest act of rebellion, I had moved across the country after college. Most of my cousins and family friends had moved back into their parents' homes after college – the Indian way. Here I was paving my own path again.

When I stopped to think about it, I was treading in my mom's well-worn path. My mom has two older sisters who married in their teens. In 1960s India, few women went to college, and if they did, they were not poor village girls. My mom went to college in the sprawling metropolis of Bombay. I had some trepidation of moving to San Francisco on my own and that is nowhere near the size of Bombay. She did not consider herself fearless; she was simply smart. She earned her degree in Economics (just as I did). None of my aunts had college degrees, but my mom never flaunted her education. Sometimes, we are both humble to a fault.

After graduating, she married my father. Soon after, my dad moved to the U.S. to start his job, but my mom was now pregnant and stayed behind to wait for her visa call. The call came as she was in the hospital giving birth to my brother, and she would have to wait almost a year for the next call. During this time, my mom moved in with my dad's parents. That year was not easy and still stands as a great testament to my mom's poise and character. She was away from her family for the first time in her

"Independent" mother and daughter in India.

life and her new husband was thousands of miles away. It was a time when in-laws expected unquestioned obedience from their daughter-in-law. My mom remained a dutiful daughter-in-law. Although her independence may have been stifled, she developed a diplomacy and resolve that would serve her well in life.

My mom, at a mature twenty-four, traveled to the U.S. with my brother to rejoin my father. A year later, I was born. Soon after, my parents began an entrepreneurial business venture while I was still in diapers. My dad, to his forward-thinking credit, recognized that my mom was his equal. She now was a full-time business partner while managing the home. It was a long, arduous road, but her perseverance paid off.

My mom did not circumvent the Indian way as I am able to do today. She followed it and then extended the boundaries so that my path would be easier to take. She's the reason I'm "too independent." How could her daughter be anything less?

Alpa Patel

Mapping Love
(for Rosalind Tuana)

It began with a map.

Life does not come with a detailed road map. Its blessings and misfortunes often catch us by surprise and we have no way to gauge the distance we must travel between destinations.

Mom would not travel. Her growing agoraphobia kept her from her dream trip back to her family homeland in Italy. But when my husband could not join me on a lecture trip across New Zealand, love overcame her anxiety, and my mother became my travel companion and helper for her nine-month-old grandson.

Unlike life, New Zealand's roadways are clearly demarcated. Mom always wanted to be involved and contribute. Since driving on the "other" side of the road was too much for her, I handed Mom a roadmap so she could navigate as we traveled across the North Island.

Our two-week adventure was filled with laughter and delight. We explored Maori culture and cuisine, my mother open to every new experience. We laughed as we warmed ourselves at geothermal vents as we explored the rugged and steam-filled landscape of Rotorua. We delighted in my dear baby; his face filled with wonder as he crawled from seashell to seashell during his first ocean experience or took his first halting steps in our hotel room at night. And we drove from bakery to bakery in search of those meat pies Mom so loved.

She could not use the map.

We do not pay attention to the first signs. The agoraphobia seemed simply the result of the isolation of retirement. And we compensate. Each night, while she was playing with my son, I would memorize the directions for the next day's journey. That way, as she fumbled to read the map, I could guide her and help her navigate without her knowledge that I was doing so. And each day I would praise her for her success in finding our destination.

I did not realize that I was learning a life lesson and beginning a pattern that would continue for more than a decade. As her dementia slowly eroded her life skills, I became my mother's navigator, helping her find her way and praising her successes. Her journey took her from me even while she was living in my home.

It was my own children who provided a map. They ignored all the changes and losses and saw only their beloved Noni whose eyes still shone with love whenever she saw them. They simply loved her – both for who she had been and for who she was.

Their love illuminated my path.

Nancy Tuana

Our Last Road Trip

In September of 2003, my mom and I went on our last road trip together. We had gone on countless family vacations with my dad and brother – many of them wonderful – but there was something special about the "just us" trips.

Our trips started when I was a sophomore in high school and my cousin was studying in Grenoble, France. "I think we should visit Kim during the kids' February vacation," Mom said one night at dinner.

"I feel like we were just there ... " my dad replied (we had gone once, three years before).

"I'd rather go someplace warm," my brother concurred.

I said nothing. Mom and I locked eyes across the kitchen table, slow smiles spreading across our faces. Our plan was hatched.

We met Kim in Paris, saw the Eiffel Tower, lingered in the Musée de l'Orangerie, and shopped at Printemps. After a few days in the city, we rented a car to take my cousin back to Grenoble. We dropped her off and took our time driving back to Paris, taking in the French countryside, just the two of us.

In my senior year of high school, I tried unsuccessfully to convince a few friends to go to Florida during our winter break.

"I wish I could go somewhere warm," I complained to my mom one evening as we sat at the top of the stairs folding laundry together.

"Well, I'll go with you ... " she said slowly, hopefully, as if she wasn't sure that I would want her to. I hadn't even thought of it – but again, the smiles spread.

Stepping off the plane into that hot, humid Florida air felt wonderful after months of being cold. We stayed a week with my grandfather in Fort Meyers – lying by the pool, swimming, taking long walks, playing tennis, playing double solitaire, and reading at night – a quiet and relaxing trip, just the two of us.

There was something wonderful about traveling with my mom. She loved being "away," loved eating out at nice restaurants, loved to say "Calories and prices don't count when you are on vacation." She was an ideal traveling companion in that very little annoyed her or worried her. "Hey – we're on vacation; it could be worse!" she would say if flights were delayed or connections missed. She knew how to relax, knew how to enjoy. She never let the little things get to her.

Traveling together gave us the gift of long stretches of uninterrupted time to talk – on a plane or in a car or while walking around a new city. We'd talk about our memories of the past, but more often she wanted to know what was going on with me in the present. She was a careful and empathetic listener, quick to ask more questions, slow to offer advice. She always wanted to know what I thought about something. Particularly as I got older, we were able to discuss things as two friends rather than as mother and daughter, and I grew to admire even more her character and strength.

And her humor. We laughed a lot on these trips. Mom always said she didn't consider herself to be funny, and she frequently told me that my behavior was "silly," but despite her protesting, she was always suspiciously quick to join in the fun. Something or another would inevitably set us off and we'd be laughing until our stomachs hurt. "Honestly, Laura," she used to say after such a fit, "you are so silly."

For her fifty-fifth birthday in 2003, I surprised her with a "just us" trip to Newport, Rhode Island. I was in my mid-twenties, living in Beacon Hill in Boston, and she picked me up there early on a September Saturday. I had a jam-packed itinerary for us – we spent the first day at a winery tasting various wines and walking among the green vineyards that rolled down to the sparkling ocean. We stayed at a small bed and breakfast and had dinner at an old, stately seaside inn a few miles outside of town. The roads leading there were dark and windy and our car, with the two of us inside, felt small next to the vast ocean.

The next day, we walked the Cliff Walk under bright sunshine, examining some of the famous mansions as we went. As lunchtime neared, we decided we should head back to Boston. We were tooling along on a coastal highway, feeling the sun on our faces, Mom at the wheel and me counting the big puffy clouds in the sky.

"You hungry?" Mom asked.

"I could eat," I replied.

Suddenly the car veered violently right to an alternate coastal route.

"Whoa, Nelly!" I exclaimed.

"Sorry," she laughed. "I saw a fork and knife on that sign."

"Well then, I guess the whiplash was worth it," I replied, breaking into a belly laugh.

We found a strange little restaurant across the street from a marina. Inside, it had been painted different shades of tropical blues and greens with murals of fish and fishing nets hung up here and there. It would have blended right in were it a bar in the Caribbean, but on the coast of Rhode Island, it was an oddity. We liked it.

A waitress brought us the menus and we began perusing.

"On an afternoon like this, here with my daughter, I think a glass of wine is in order," Mom declared with a smile.

The waitress came over and took our order. She left and we looked at one another, happy for the time we had spent, but a bit sad also, knowing that our weekend was coming to an end.

She reached across the table and put her hand on mine. Her hand was warm and soft – a hand I had held more times in my life than I could count.

"Thank you," she said. "This was the best birthday present I could have."

I smiled at her, my eyes and heart full. I couldn't respond.

We both looked out the window again at the empty coastal road and the ocean beyond. We were the only people in the restaurant. It was just us.

Laura Souza

The author's mother, Nancy Ellen Shea, passed away after a six-year battle with cancer in September of 2004. She was fifty-six years old.

SECTION THREE

Snapshots, Photographs, and Portraits

From below her bedroom window she heard voices, and looking out she saw her mother standing in the grass, her arms crossed on her chest. She seemed very small, and Maggie felt as if she were looking at her through the wrong end of a telescope. She realized that these days she was always seeing her mother from a distance, as if in pictures – framed in a window, frozen in some pose, her face revealed in some essential way. Just yesterday she had come silently into the dining room on bare feet and seen Connie through the door leading to the kitchen, leaning back against the counter, flushed and radiant. Maggie had suddenly thought that her mother looked beautiful, young ... Then Maggie had moved, and her mother had moved, and the moment had been over.

Anna Quindlen
Object Lessons

Unpacking

In the end, a home is made of small things.

The house my partner and I signed the papers for in State College, Pennsylvania five years ago was the first either of us had owned. We're the kind of people who burrow down into a place once we've found it. We both long for a sense of rootedness. I had lived for twenty-eight years in one house in Cape Town and then a series of flats as a student before moving to the U.S., and he had rented various places in New York, San Francisco, and then in State College. The house we bought is a simple and clear space. In these five years we've gradually been turning it into a sanctuary.

Making a home is a long process, and on that scale five years is almost nothing. We sent for our boxes from storage in California and they arrived in a giant moving truck. During the six hours it took to unload everything, the drivers, Juan and Charlie, played 1980s music that reverberated down the street. I was secretly pleased by how many of the songs I could still sing.

Juan and Charlie carried the impossibly heavy bureaus and cabinets through the wide door of the house, and we made suddenly permanent decisions about where to put them because we would never be able to move them again. When they were done and the street became quiet again, there was a myriad of boxes in every room. We unpacked slowly and then in a fever.

Out came all the ordinary parts of a house – cutlery, cords for our computers, books – and also the heart-stopping recollection of when we'd last used them. D lingered over his mother's favorite books and his father sketchbooks. Unwrapping the newspaper and bubble-wrap from old bowls reminded me of having left Cape Town, my suitcase carefully packed, my mother there to ensure that whatever was precious and fragile was buffered by layers of clothing. D's mother too had layered all her beautiful linens with tissue. We unpacked all these memories too.

The paintings were the most magical of all. The redwood paneling in the small house proved a perfect setting for hanging the landscapes D's father had painted years before. Bright red suns striped by blue clouds settled like sunsets over my desk. Cool blue morning suns edged with pale mauve greeted us in the morning at the dining room table. The fireplace was crowned by a yellow sun with green and purple clouds. Everything was finding its place.

I too was slowly fitting in. On a trip to Sweden, I found three glass bowls that exactly matched the mauve sun in D's father's painting and his mother's tablecloth with the green and blue embroidery in the living room. Setting them on the table, I felt that something of mine had knitted with something of theirs.

Most poignant of all was a cluster of D's baby photos that his mother had gathered together. There he was in her arms, with his brother, on the baby chair about to eat, growing, becoming the man I would meet. Then it struck me. I had simply been adding to our house rather than helping to shape it. I wanted to grow my roots here, my own beginning and becoming. I unpacked my baby photos, protected by layers of soft scarves in my suitcase by my mother, and put them next to D's. Me in my mother's arms. Me looking gravely out at the camera. They are small likenesses, almost unnoticeable, but when I walk past them I feel time stretch deep into the house.

Gabeba Baderoon

Tomato Soup ... A Silver Moon

My grandmother, Doris Elaine Perkins, was not part of the "me" generation. Selflessly, she took care of others including raising me long after she had reared her own two sons. Without hesitation, when my parents divorced, she made time for me and I went to live with her. At that stage in her life, she was a saleswoman in the fine china and silver department of a high-end store – each day dressing smartly in one of those curve-fitting dresses of the fifties, decked out in pearls and pumps. She gave up the glamour of high style and milkshakes at the lunch counter with friends so her granddaughter would have a grown-up at home at noon (as most kids did in those days). From first grade through eighth grade, she was there with tomato soup and a sandwich waiting for me every single day.

My grandmother – I called her Nan – was the one who would sit up and wait for her sons, for me, for her friends. She was the best listener. She put no limits on me climbing into bed next to her, any night that I needed to. There was nothing so comforting to me in all the world.

For my Nan, loving and following God's teachings was a joy. Throughout her life she needed her deep faith to carry her. She worried and prayed for the safety and health of her two boys all of their lives. Nan's strength served her well through the death of her husband Charles who was the love of her life, and the middle-age deaths of her sons, Stanley and Wayne.

Because she was always home, Nan would care for her neighbor's animals. Roxy and Pepper were a big part of her life. I worried about Pepper's health because her belly almost dragged on the floor. I'd say, "Isn't that dog on a diet?" Nan would dismiss me and give the dog another taste of whatever she was eating.

Joyfulness was her attitude toward all household duties. She used an old wringer washing machine to wash my clothes and then she would hang them on the line. I never washed a dish. She'd say, "You go play! There'll be time enough for washing dishes."

I'd play in the attic and sing. She'd tell me how pretty my songs were. I'd draw pictures and she made me feel like a child prodigy showing them off to her friends.

Nan made time for me. She read to me and quizzed me on the multiplication table. She is the reason I made it through school and graduated from college. She taught me to love the moon when it was shining over the harbor just outside our window.

I moved away to New York with my mother at the age of thirteen, just before my grandfather retired, but I'd return to this safe haven every summer. I'd come back to lobster bakes, bonfires on the beach, the little white painted church, feeling welcome all over again in her sweet community of Dipper Harbor, a little north of Maine.

Nan would want me to go with her to visit her neighbor across the harbor. We'd drive over to see Grace, but we couldn't visit Grace without stopping to see Kay. Next we'd be paying a dooryard call to every friend within a ten-mile radius, including the postal lady. She'd introduce me again and again, beaming all the while. That was my Nan!

When my children and I visited several summers ago, they were eleven and seven. I went out for a jog around the harbor, leaving them with Nan. Dayna and Danny were out in the sun porch and Danny was playing with the old skeleton key in the door lock to the main house. The door to outside from this room was nailed shut. Danny jiggled the key and it broke in the lock. Dayna banged on the window to get Nan's attention. Nan walked over and Danny motioned to indicate that they were locked in the sun porch, but Nan just said, "Don't play with the lock," and turned and left. The kids looked at each other helplessly.

I returned an hour later to find them banging on the door to get my attention. They pointed to the couch. Nan was snoozing. Danny was jumping up and down holding himself because he had to pee. Nan didn't really understand any part of the whole episode. Her mind was beginning to slip.

On my last night with her in her final illness, I'd gone back to her room three times to see her and to say one more final good-bye. After I had climbed on the bed with her for the third time, she told me that I needed to go. I was trying not to cry in front of her. At that time her body was frail and giving out, but her deep awareness and sensitivity were still strong. I held her delicate hand, all spotted thin white skin, and she said, "It's dark and foggy; you have a long ride." In the soft but firm voice of a parent she said, "Now go!" We both knew it was probably the last moment for us. She was using her own inner strength to enable me to leave her because I was failing miserably. One of life's sad, sad, knowing moments is when you force your feet to move away from someone you love that you are losing.

Later that night, at a rest stop on the drive to Bangor, I was eating French fries and I started sobbing. The memories of fish-and-chip Fridays with Doris and Charles, my dear grandparents – my caregivers and life-savers – overwhelmed me. The fries made me homesick and lonely for them. My salty tears fell on my salty fries. I wanted to bury my face in my grandfather's shirt and smell him again; to go back briefly to the time in my life when I was a young girl, so lucky to have their attention and love. My grandmother was always, always there, just as it seems to children that a school teacher never leaves school but stays day and night until they walk in the classroom the next morning.

Nan taught me something about strength and love and things that matter like appreciating a silver thin crescent moon on a clear night when the sky is black. If you really look carefully, you can see the whole round magnificent rock on those nights. It's always there, just like my Nan, and that's what matters.

Cindy Carubia

Reflections on a Life Well Lived

My mom died recently; about a month after her ninetieth birthday. During the two weeks between that last stroke and her death, my brother Jim and I sat with her in her bedroom, holding her hand, reliving memories, and feeling the warmth of her love, her strength and her grace. Of all the gifts she gave us over the years, the intimacy of those two weeks was one of the most meaningful and beautiful.

On several occasions during that time, we phoned my cousin Betty, daughter of my mom's sister Mary, to tell her how her beloved Aunt Jane was doing. During one call, my brother asked Betty what were her earliest memories of our mom. Without hesitation, she painted us this picture:

During the war, when Betty was a child, her mother, Mary, contracted tuberculosis. While she was recovering in a far-away sanatorium, Betty lived with her mother's family – Mary's parents, her two sisters (my mom and her younger sister Ruth), her brother Max, and her aunt Gimpy. Jane and Ruth were young adults at the time and apparently quite fashionable – Jane sewed all of her own clothes and in photos taken by my dad when they were courting, she looks like a model.

Betty reminisced to us that one day the two classy sisters were getting ready to go out. They put on leg make-up – nylons were not available during the war – and then Ruth stood up on a chair. Jane proceeded to draw "seams" down the back of her legs with an eyeliner pencil! Betty's shared memory brought joy and laughter to Jim and me as we returned with lightened hearts to our vigil at my mom's bedside. What a picture!

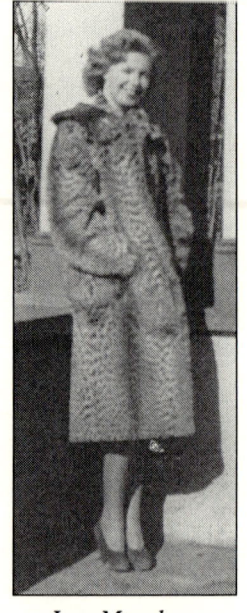

Jane Manahan Balmer, circa 1940. A beautiful woman inside and out.

Now as I look back, I see more than the antics of two young women in this vivid image. It also reminds me of my mom's creativity – she could always make something beautiful and unique from whatever she had at hand, and she found happiness and fulfillment in doing so. Over the years, she crafted valentines, family celebrations, gifts, and treats for her kids, and then for her grandson. She made presents for countless friends and their children. Her quiet joy in life came from giving to others and making the most of every moment. How I miss my mother and how I cherish these memories!

Joanne Balmer Green

An Irish Lady

On my bedroom dresser, I have a photo of the only grandmother I ever knew (my dad's mother died when he was young). She's about nineteen years old. An elaborate hat and a coat with a stand-up collar frame her young face and beautifully coiffed hair.

Born in 1877, in Arklow, County Wicklow, Ireland, Kate Manifold came to St. Paul, Minnesota, at the age of eight. Her family settled in the West Side flats, along with other Irish immigrants. At fourteen she took a job painting lard cans for a paint firm, working nine hours a day, six days a week, for two dollars. That's where she met her future husband, Frank Whaley, who was driving a truck for the same company. That photo on my dresser may have been her formal engagement photo.

Grandma Whaley in 1896.

By the time they married, Frank was head baggage agent at the St. Paul Union Depot. At first, they lived on Congress Street in a house that was a gift from her mother, who by then owned several houses and gave one to each daughter as she got married. She bore eight children, losing the first when he was twenty-one years old and the last at birth. In 1915, the year my mother was born, Frank built a large house on the West Side, to accommodate their growing family. He said to her, "You wanted a house. I'll give you a mansion."

During World War II, when my dad knew he would probably have to go to war, our parents, my twin sister, and I moved into that "mansion." The upper floor had been turned into an apartment for us. Grandma Whaley was sixty-five years old then, and my sister and I were four. In my memory, she always looked the same: brown hair streaked with a little grey and arranged up in a bun, knee-length dresses, lisle stockings (silk on Sundays), and sensible shoes. She was only out of costume when she donned long cotton pants or the occasional bathing suit at the lake cottage where the family spent their summers. After we moved out of the apartment and Grandpa retired, she had her "handiwork"

47

to keep her busy. She taught us how to embroider – painstakingly doing cross-stitches on a towel or an apron. She also showed us how to do an Irish jig.

My most vivid memories of her have to do with food. In summers when we would visit at their lake cottage, she would be shelling peas or cooking and serving the stream of people who showed up regularly – the more the merrier. At home, she canned peaches, tomatoes, and green beans. She also put up applesauce and rhubarb sauce from the bounty growing in the back yard.

At Christmastime, she made plum pudding. I keep a copy of her handwritten recipe in my own recipe folder. On it she wrote, "I would get the bread a few weeks ahead and let it get good and stale, and then I would put it in the food chopper and grind it." After everything was prepared, she would steam it for eleven hours in the basement, using the burner and tub normally reserved for the Monday wash.

During the holidays, she also baked countless loaves of Barm Brack, the Irish fruit bread. In a note to a friend about making this bread, she wrote that she used potato water for her sponge. "My sponge would fill my big pot, my bread would raise, so I would have to get up several times to punch it down. It is a lot of work, believe me. I loved to make it. I never cared how often I got out of bed at night. The good smell was in the house the day I made the bread."

She didn't use a cookbook. When I asked how she made biscuits, for instance, she said, "Add the flour until it feels right." On Thanksgiving, she invariably chose the neck as her favorite part of the turkey, probably because that was all that was left by the time she sat down to eat.

Grandma had a lot of little sayings that we thought were original, such as: "If wishes were horses, beggars would ride." "There's no accounting for taste, said Mrs. Murphy as she kissed the cow." Speaking of visitors, she would say, "Relatives and fish begin to smell after three days." If the carrots were not cooked enough, she would say they were "cunning." "Little pitchers have big ears," she warned, when the adults were having a private conversation as children hung about the kitchen.

If she had a fault, it was that she unfailingly catered to the men, starting with her husband – perhaps a fallback to her Irish-Catholic heritage or simply the age in which she lived. The daughters made their brothers' beds. The boys went to college; the girls did not. My twin sister still remembers the time when we, aged twelve, our parents, and five-year-old brother visited them for supper and Grandma served the men, including our little brother, in the dining room, while the ladies ate in the kitchen.

She was a compliant wife, a confidante to her children, and a buffer to Grandpa Frank's stern paternal style. In my own mother's memory, if a child had a request or a problem, Grandma would mention it to him as she passed the potatoes at supper. When she was seventy-one and he was seventy-three, Grandpa Frank died, and her hair, which had been mostly brown, turned grey almost overnight.

The word that comes to mind when I think of her is "ladylike." She always stood upright. She never crossed her legs. She always looked neat and well put-together. And she liked being busy. Well into her eighties she would take a bus to our family house in a north suburb of St. Paul and ask my mom what she could do – most often the ironing.

Her mind stayed clear, but her body finally gave out at age ninety-five. Sadly, she never made it back to Arklow, County Wicklow. But we've been there twice and have learned a great deal about the Manifolds and the origins of Katherine Manifold Whaley's loving and generous Irish spirit.

In addition to her photograph on my dresser, and those recipes for plum pudding and Barm Brack, I have in my kitchen her black and blue enameled sieve, which I use regularly; an iron mold for baking an Easter cake in the shape of a lamb; and a pot in which she used to make Irish stew. Some traits I may have inherited from her are her willingness to help and care for others, her traditionalism, and her love of having people around and cooking pots of things for them to eat.

Annette Conklin

My Mother's Flesh

In the hospital, finally,
She needed me, her daughter.

She let me lift
the thin, light cotton gown
to uncover what had been hidden
my whole life:
the thighs, belly, and buttocks
of my mother.

I had dreaded that moment,
to see the flesh she had told me for years
was ugly and fat,
veined and pale.
She wouldn't go swimming or wear shorts;
she was living out the myth of the hag,
the crone;
the weeping out of beauty and worth in
a woman's fullest years of wisdom.

Men had taken the stronghold of her womanhood easily,
"Those things are just a nuisance; I don't need them now,"
she said, coming around the corner
so abruptly that her voice broke into shards of irony.

Under the gown, I finally saw the simple
clear beauties of her shape and skin:
lucid and smooth,
marked delicately with the cartographer's blue ink,
swelling and folding in cadences
completely outside the limits of
aesthetic judgment.
Beautiful only because beauty is.

In the mirror, I see her flesh hung
less gracefully on my bones.

Once, I saw my mother's flesh,
but now, I need to see
her soul.

Josephine Carubia

My Mother as a Woman

My mother died in the spring of 1950 at the age of thirty-three, when I was not yet nine years old, my brother not yet seven, and my sister only nine months old.

The sixty years since have, of course, eroded many memories that never had a chance either to form or to gel. A lot of the memories and attendant images have a multisensory fuzziness about them: riding in the backseat of a car that she was driving, enduring her steady resistance to my stubborn refusal to wear galoshes with knickers, the competent wrapping of my hand that had been ripped open by hitting a hidden stump while dangerously riding on a sled in the forest off the trail. I am both inside and outside these scenarios.

The most persistent and recurring memory I have of her is from a summer day at the Dreamland Swimming Pool in Huntington, West Virginia, a memory of a scenario in which I was definitely "on the outside." Looking up from the child's side of the pool to a table higher up from pool level where she sat with some of her friends, *I saw my mother as a woman.*

At that moment, she had nothing to do with me; did not belong to me at all. I saw that she belonged to that gathering around the table, a group of women talking and sipping iced tea together. It was a strangely objective experience, a registering of a fact about my mother and a recognition of her place in another circle.

Of course, I never had the chance to say anything about this to my mother. I did not know it had to be said or even could be said. Maybe that is why the photo of her smiling face, with no premonition of mortality, that rests on the desk in our living room does not just remind me of a loss but is a manifestation of what she both was and was not to be.

Robert E. Innis

SECTION FOUR

The Great and The Grand

We are volcanoes. When we women offer our experience as our truth, as human truth, all the maps change. There are new mountains.

Ursula LeGuin

Flora

My grandfather was upstairs sleeping; he was working the night shift at the mill that week, so he slept until supper time. Uncle Elmer was mowing grass on his Graveley tractor. It was mid-afternoon and my grandmother had just finished putting the roast in the oven. She and I were sitting at her kitchen table peeling potatoes and carrots. I wanted to ask her again about my great-grandmother Flora whose photo was on a table in the back parlor. Flora was my grandfather's mother, but my grandmother had lived in the same house with her in-laws since her marriage in 1924. She had known Flora well.

"Grandma, please tell me the cheese story about grandpap's mother," I begged. "It's my favorite."

The peeler stopped for a bit, and my grandmother smiled as she began telling the story.

***

Flora was feisty. The whole family knew it: your great-grandfather and your grandpa and Uncle Elmer, Uncle Earl, Uncle Ernie, and Aunt Flora who was named after her. So on the day of the annual Fourth of July picnic one year, no one was surprised when she came downstairs in red, white, and blue bloomers and patriotic streamers entwined in her thick, graying hair, pulled up into a loose knot.

Flora's face was broad, ethnic-looking; more Eastern European-looking than the Scotch ancestry she claimed as a MacDonald, her parents having come over on the boat in the late 1800s. Her nose was large and hooked, but her eyes were big and bright and clear blue, like the roadside chicory or the sky early on a summer morning. Flora's smile was a sly one, saved for moments when she knew she had triumphed. Like the time a visitor had too much to drink, and passed out. She rolled him inside the porch rug and left him there all night. When she had finished rolling him into the rug, she smiled. Her laugh could range from a chuckle to raucous guffaws. She even slapped her knee every now and again when she laughed so hard that the tears rolled down her face.

She was a stocky woman, not tall, but ample, as was the term in fashion at the time. Flora looked more as if she should be out in the field with a plow, not taking care of a house, five children, and a husband. She dressed plainly. With all those mouths to feed on a mill worker's salary, she didn't have much left to spend on finery.

Flora made the bloomers she wore that day, sewing red and blue stars onto a pair of her old white bloomers that she had bleached and hung in the sun until they didn't look so old anymore. The stars covered up the worn places. And what fun to be the only one daring enough to wear bloomers to the picnic!

Your grandpap's family had been celebrating the Fourth of July together for twenty or so years, ever since his parents had purchased the farmhouse and sixteen acres atop Memory Lane. It was a perfect spot for a picnic with rolling green lawn, pine trees, elms, horse chestnuts, catalpas, and oaks. And a big field that your Uncle Elmer mowed once a year so the men and boys could play softball. Everyone ate on wooden tables and chairs out on the lawn, up under the oak and locust trees. Nothing fancy: ham sandwiches, potato salad, homegrown green beans if they were ready, and watermelon or peach cobbler for dessert. Flora had canned the peaches the past August from the fruit trees at the end of their property.

Flora drew the line at alcohol though. No liquor or beer would be served in her house, inside or out. She made a delicious fruit punch and there was always plenty of cold, well water to drink. Her father had been a drinker, so she knew – and besides, she could make her own fun; she didn't need drink to help!

She was up early that Fourth of July, as she was every day. But that day she had to feed thirty hungry relatives, so she was up extra early. She made a quick breakfast for her family and then shooed them all outside to set up tables and chairs and put up red, white, and blue crepe streamers all along her clothesline, which ran the length of the walk. The streamers had been on sale at G. C. Murphy's last year after the Fourth of July, and she had been wise to buy them then because the price that next year was just ridiculous. They looked rather lovely in her hair, she must have thought, as she had looked into the vanity mirror that morning. The boys would hang flags from the porch railing and a few of the tree limbs, too.

All the windows and doors in the house were open. A hint of a breeze swayed through the kitchen, gently rustling the streamers in her hair. She hummed a Sousa march to herself. It would be another hot one; that was for sure.

The men arrived in dress shirts, but quickly stripped down to their undershirts to play ball and horseshoes and smoke cigars. The women, in their nicest outfits, would spend the day under the trees, catching up, laughing at the men, and exchanging gossip. Flora wasn't much for gossip. She much preferred to sit with the men and talk politics and the mill. But she was a good hostess, so she sat with the women.

The children were left to fend for themselves on the Fourth, the older ones taking charge of their younger siblings and any other children within eyesight.

Your mother was one of the older children who liked to play with the young ones. I guess that is why she made such a good schoolteacher.

No one in Flora's family was still alive, so everyone at the picnic came from your great-grandfather's side of the family; wild Irishmen who made a living in the mill doing hot and dangerous work. Their wives were a lively lot once, too, but were hampered now with children and housework and making ends meet.

Right after lunch, Flora made the potato salad in a cast iron roast pan that had belonged to her mother-in-law. Uncles, aunts, and cousins began arriving so they could get in a few good games of softball before supper. Horseshoes was more of a twilight game that could be played on bloated, full stomachs. The horseshoes would fly through the air, clanging on the poles at each end, sometimes making a spark fly, although it may have been a firefly, too. There were hundreds of them roaming above the grass, casting their fluorescent twinkles on the game.

Flora hoped that Sam didn't come this year. Every year he caused some sort of trouble. Sam was your great-grandfather's fourth cousin, or some distant relation like that. He worked at odd jobs only when he needed money for drink, and he left his wife and six children to get by as best they could. He never brought them to the picnic. Flora wasn't sure that Sam had even been invited. He would just appear.

As we all sat down to supper in the waning afternoon under the welcome coolness of the trees, someone at another table yelled that Sam was coming up the hill. He pumped the men's hands and kissed the women's cheeks as he made room for himself at a crowded table. He didn't dare sit with Flora. When he shouted a hearty "Amen" as your great-grandfather finished saying grace, we knew this year would be no different. Sam was back. Without even getting near him (he hadn't dared to kiss her with the look she had on her face), Flora knew he would smell of whiskey, or maybe beer if he hadn't worked in a while.

After dinner Sam let out a belch that Flora heard four tables away. The women turned their heads while the men tried not to snicker. The children were giggling.

Sam was ruining it all, again. He had tried to pitch horseshoes after supper but was so unsteady on his feet that the men made him sit down in the grass and watch. Miffed, he came around the house to sit with the women. He could be charming when he wanted to be or when he wanted something.

As it was getting darker and after the horseshoes ended, everyone usually sat in a circle on the front lawn to sing old melodies, hymns, or patriotic tunes. It was a sweet time of togetherness for the family, even if only once a year, just as it still is. The children sat on the grass, catching lightning bugs as they flew through the circle, listening to their parents' voices, some of them amazingly good. Stomachs were full, muscles were tired, and hearts were reaching out.

Not this year, though. As evening rose up around them, Sam was up out of his seat, swaying around the middle of the circle singing a bawdy song. He was staggering and almost fell several times; the drink and the twirling making him dizzy. Several of the men, including your great-grandfather, stepped into the circle to help him back to a chair. He shrugged them off and began singing anew, these lyrics more lewd than the last.

When he pulled the flask out of his pocket, Flora had had enough. She stood up, signaled to your great-grandfather, and each took an arm and hoisted Sam across the lawn, over to the front porch, where he collapsed on the porch swing, legs splayed, the flask dangling from his limp hand. He had finally passed out.

Your great-grandfather saw a sly smile pass over Flora's face. "She's up to something," he thought," but who could really blame her? She ducked in the kitchen door and reemerged in a few seconds with something in her hand. The porch was dark so he couldn't make out what it was except that it was a rather large lump. Flora broke whatever it was in half, and your great-grandfather knew immediately.

She reached into Sam's two trouser pockets and deposited a lump in each, patting the pockets for good measure. By this time, your great-grandfather had left the porch, driven away by the smell. Flora flashed her special smile as she wiped the remaining Limburger cheese from her hands into Sam's lap. Sam wouldn't be back. She was sure of it!

***

I laughed as I always did when I heard that story, and others, about my great-grandmother Flora. My grandmother laughed with me as we sliced the potatoes and carrots. Grandpap and Uncle Elmer would want their dinner soon.

Laurie Mansell Reich

Sweet Haven

You who have journeyed the wide world through
Knowing the Old World as the New,
Cruise or pilgrimage or shrine,
Found you ever so all-divine
A haven as first was yours and mine
Out to old Aunt Mary's?

It all comes back so clear to-day!
Though I am as bald as you are gray,
Out by the barn-lot and down the lane
We patter along in the dust again,
As light as the tips of the drops of the rain,
Out to old Aunt Mary's.

And the romps we took, in our glad unrest!
Was it the lawn that we loved the best,
With its swooping swing in the locust trees,
Or was it the grove, with its leafy breeze,
Or the dim hay-mow, with its fragrancies
Out to old Aunt Mary's.

But home, with Aunty in nearer call,
That was the best place, after all!
The talks on the back-porch, in the low
Slanting sun and the evening glow,
With the voice of counsel that touched us so,
Out to old Aunt Mary's.

And then in the dust of the road again;
And the teams we met, and the countrymen;
And the long highway, with sunshine spread
As thick as butter on country bread,
Our cares behind, and our hearts ahead
Out to old Aunt Mary's.

And as many a time have you and I
Barefoot boys in the days gone by
Knelt, and in tremulous ecstasies
Dipped our lips into sweets like these,
Memory now is on her knees
Out to old Aunt Mary's.

James Whitcomb Riley

Optimism

When I was a child, the six of us lived in a two-bedroom apartment in Hamburg, Germany. It was very simple; we had no shower or tub, just a toilet and a sink in the bathroom.

I never knew my mother's mother. My father's mother was the only grandmother I ever knew. She always seemed old, old, old. I don't remember her young. What I do remember is that every time we got a present, she came to the house and sneaked it out and shipped it to eastern Germany. One time I came home from school and my doll was gone. I only had that one doll and she took it away from me. When we asked for our toys back, she said, "They are now with children who are very, very poor." But we were poorer than poor ourselves! Nobody knew where she was sending the toys. It was someone from her side of the family, perhaps her brother and his children.

I had an aunt, my father's sister, cut from the same cloth who promised me socks every year. I am now sixty-five years old and I have never seen a pair of socks from her. This is something a child will remember, a promise made over and over, but never fulfilled. All of this must have affected my mother, too, but she kept us going and kept us happy. If it wasn't for her positive spirit, I wouldn't be sitting here.

Mother with her four children.

My mother was the rock in the family. She was always optimistic. She said, "If someone does something bad, they will be punished for it someday." When we felt hurt by unkind actions, she said, "Don't worry about that; they will be punished! You just stay optimistic and happy!" I got that from her. My son Florian is also that same way.

When we kids were babies, Hitler's government gave our family a nanny and other support for child rearing. A family got a nanny when they had four or more children. Mama qualified for this help because the four of us were born between 1939 and 1944. Those were the war years, of course, so it was very difficult having babies and trying to take good care of a young family. My father's alcoholism made everything just that much worse. A terribly sad incident happened before I was born when my brother Peter was lost during the war when he was just six months old.

My mother had to bring my sister, Karin, to her mother in Konigsberg which is in East Prussia. Karin would turn blue and couldn't breathe when she heard the alarms warning of an imminent bombing attack. My mother would have to revive her over and over again, so she wanted to take her out of the city. It wasn't much better in Konigsberg because they had no food and were begging from door to door. While my mother was traveling with Karin, she left baby Peter with a friend. This woman had her own child as well. One day, she had the two babies out in the park and there was an alarm. She left my brother and the stroller in the park when she ran to safety with her own child.

They found the stroller, empty and burned, after the bombing attack. They had no clue what happened to the baby. It took my mother six months to find her baby son. She was able to identify him in an orphanage because Peter had a distinctive little bone spur behind his ear. We believe something happened to him during the bombing because he was never the same. He seemed unharmed physically, but he remained cognitively disabled and very childlike his whole life.

When I was about three or four years old and the war was finally over, she sent us to a day nursery so she could go back to work. It was a humongous building with programs for the children of parents who were working. Families only needed to pay as much as they could afford.

Mother came home and cooked dinner for us if we had money for dinner. I remember as a little child going to bed hungry. One job she had reminds me of the story where Cinderella is separating the good from the bad grains. My mother had a job separating coffee beans. When she had enough of that, she worked in a fish-processing factory. She wore great big boots, and she came home smelling terrible. Finally, she got the right job. She worked for thirty years as a trolley driver. She loved it and so did I. I would have free rides on the trolley. She took the tickets and she was also the driver. This job had good conditions, health insurance, and that uniform with silver buttons. I remember that she also had an apron with a coin changer.

My mother asked for a divorce two or three times, but Father came back each time promising to be better. After six months, things would be the same as before. When I was a child I was frightened by his tirades, and I would open all the windows in our apartment so everyone could hear my father yelling. Some of the neighbors would then call the police.

My sisters and I all married early because we wanted to get away from our father. When he was dying, my father told my sister Heidi that he wanted to tell me something. At that moment, I was on vacation at the North Sea and she drove all the way there to get me, but by the time we got back to him, he was gone. I never knew for sure what he wanted to tell me, but I think he wanted to say he was sorry that he gave all of us such a miserable childhood. I was his favorite child, and I think he could say these words only to me.

After my father died in 1966, my mother began to live. She moved out of the old apartment. She and my brother Peter lived together, and they moved into a new apartment in a new town. By this time Peter had a good job. I had driven him around in my VW to help him find him a job. After looking at many, many possibilities, Peter became a bellboy in a very famous hotel, and he loved it. Peter was very handsome, and he was an excellent bellboy. The owner of this hotel wanted to give Peter a job because he also had a child who was cognitively disabled.

Mama gained weight after my father died. Life was marvelous. She always had many friends because she was such an optimistic person. In particular, I remember her good friend, Emmy Haas. They would go out dancing, blueberry picking, cherry picking, strawberry picking, out for dinner; whatever they did, they had a marvelous time together. They were always doing something fun!

After so many years of hardship, I was glad to see my mother enjoying her life. Her optimism carried us all through hard times, tragedies, and war. I have drawn upon her positive spirit many times in my own life and I'm glad to see her optimism alive and well in my son's life. He, too, has a struggling young family. His battleground is living with the challenge of multiple sclerosis. I feel that Mama is with him every day, filling him with energy and hope.

Marina Berges

Generations

How do I begin to describe the soft, strong, flexible tapestry of life woven among women in my family? I am sixty-six years old and I am now a great grandmother myself. I have personally touched and loved seven generations of women and all are vividly part of my life every day. I am too close to the thread to tell the patterns of my own life, and my daughters, granddaughters, and great-granddaughter are still weaving their own vibrant colors into the tapestry. Let me show you some small corners of the fabric from my sister, mother, grandmother, and great grandmother that are still bright in my memory.

My Great Grandma Nettie was a very active woman. I recall that when my mother was recuperating from an operation, Great Grandma Nettie traveled two hours each way to help my mother. My sister and I were sent away to summer camp, and she was there to support my mother, her granddaughter, through a difficult time. There is a very special bond between a grandmother and granddaughters.

I always admired my grandmother Rose. She overcame adversity and accomplished many things that were extraordinary for a woman of her time. Her husband, my grandfather Alfred, was something of a tyrant. He abused her for many years, but in 1932, at the urging of my mother Nettie, who was only fourteen at the time, they separated.

A separation and divorce was a bold move at this time and in the Italian immigrant community. Grandma Rose was a seamstress and she worked hard to support her four girls. She worked so hard that by the early 1950s she owned her own factory in Brooklyn. This was not commonplace for women; in fact, it might have been one of the only woman-owned garment businesses at that time.

She was a remarkable seamstress – she made wedding dresses and bridesmaid dresses for her daughters when they married. I can recall yards and yards of fabric all over her house during these times.

Grandma Rose lived in the same three-family house where we lived when I was very young. When I was about three or four years old, I had a small doll carriage that I played with in the apartment. I would sometimes go into her apartment (next door on the same floor) to play. I would take her dish towels off the racks and cover my dolls. When I was asked why I didn't do this at home, I replied, "I don't want to mess up my mother's house." I was reminded of that story to great family delight throughout my life.

I remember going into her dress factory – which was across the street from where we all lived. My job was to put the belts on the dresses. Grandma Rose didn't work me too hard: I would put belts on dresses for about five minutes and earn a quarter. I immediately went to the candy store with my sister and spent my twenty-five cents on penny candy – I remember standing in front of the candy jars trying to make a decision as to what to get – which should it be and how many ... smarties, licorice, bubblegum, button candy (the ones on sheets of paper), waxed coke bottles. Anita and I spent a long time choosing and left with our paper sack full of candy.

One time when I was about eight years old, I went to visit Grandma Rose with my family. We did not live in the same building at this time, and she invited me to stay overnight. Since it was a Saturday, I refused because I didn't have a dress to wear to church for Sunday mass the next morning. She remarked that it was not a problem.

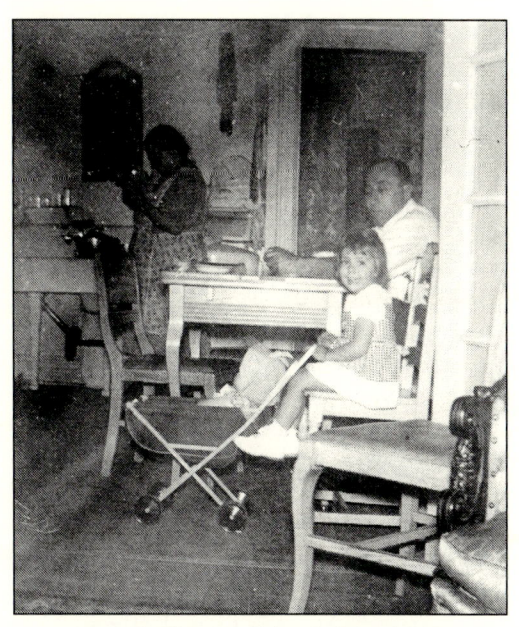

Little Roslynne with her baby carriage visiting Grandma and Papa Alessi on 13th Street in New York City.

I went to sleep and the next morning I found this beautiful mint green dress just my size with petticoats and all. The dress was embroidered at the top and bottom of the full skirt. The cap sleeves had elastic and I was able to pull them over my shoulders. I felt so grown up. It was my favorite dress for a very long time. She designed and constructed the pattern herself from brown paper bags. She must have had the fabric in the house, because she made me that dress in the hours between my bedtime and when I got up in the morning.

Occasionally, Grandma Rose had a male friend over to visit. He sometimes was there for the holidays. His name was Mr. Al Rock and he owned a nut factory. I remember that he always brought pistachios when he came to visit. I was well into my adulthood before it was brought to my attention that he was my grandmother's boyfriend. I just never put two and two together. How naïve I was!

In addition to working hard and being a pioneer in some ways, Grandma

Rose enjoyed life. She had a wonderful laugh. She loved having family over for dinners. My favorite dish of all her specialties was the nickel-size meatballs she made on holidays. This was always served with freshly minced almonds. How delicious!

Grandma Rose knew how to take care of herself, even becoming one of the first women in the area to purchase and drive her own car. The car I remember best was a 1949 Lincoln. I remember that both the front and back doors opened from the center of the car. I was with her when she sold it, but I don't remember how we got home afterward.

She also traveled to Italy several times, going first class on whatever transatlantic ship she sailed. I remember seeing pictures of her in her evening gown and silver fox coat sitting at the captain's table. She worked hard for her success and she was not afraid to spend money on herself. She knew how to enjoy her life.

My mother and my sister both inherited Grandma Rose's courage and her love of life. The courage my mother showed in taking a stand against her father came from a very difficult childhood. Grandmother Rose took the worst of it, but Alfred's daughters didn't get off easy. When he came home from work late, the children had to stay up and wait for him to have dinner. Sometimes dinner was at 11:00 p.m., and by that time the girls were sleeping with their heads on the table.

My mother never graduated from high school; she was working by the time she was fourteen. In spite of this struggle in her childhood and an incomplete education, she loved word games. She was always doing crossword puzzles. While I was growing up, she and I would spend hours playing Scrabble. It became a special game between us, a time for laughter and bonding. Neither of us played Scrabble with anyone else. After I married and moved to Long Island, I eventually found a friend who also liked to play word games. We would sometimes play Scrabble while the children were in school. It was comforting to continue this tradition, even though with another woman. By then, I was as addicted to word games as my mother.

My sister Anita was a few years older than I, and she became the keeper of all the family stories. She had the most delightful way of making the stories come to life with colorful details and a most intimate tone of voice. Everyone loved listening to her.

My most vivid memories of my sister Anita have to do with holidays. Anita loved celebrating Christmas with her family. She always invited extended family on both sides to her home for Christmas Eve. She prepared a traditional Italian meal, which included seven fish dishes.

Despite the fact that she never learned to drive, Anita went overboard buying Christmas gifts. Since she needed someone to drive her to the stores, she started her shopping early – sometimes as early as July. She would hide the gifts somewhere in the house and the children never found them. On Christmas morning her living room was filled with gifts. Anita was also generous with the rest of the family, myself included, even when we agreed not to exchange gifts. Maybe she felt I needed some special attention because I was divorced and living alone.

For several years after Anita died, I decorated my house for Christmas in her memory. My children were already grown and on their own, but surrounded by all the holiday decorations, I felt Anita's presence in my house. I still miss having Anita around to tell me our family stories.

I never stop missing and feeling grateful to all of these women. Their gifts enrich my life every single day.

Roslynne Canfield

Haantje: Johanna Johansson van den Berge

You asked for my life story; the big question is, "Where should I start?" I think the name is first on the list. My grandmother, Masamie, gave it to me. She would say, "Look at her leading the other kids around just like a little rooster (Haantje)," and it stuck. It will give you the general idea that I was a big problem in the peaceful life of the family.

From the unpublished memoir of Johanna van den Berge

***

When we remember our Oma (grandmother), Johanna Margaretha Johansson van den Berge, we remember stories. We remember them not only because she was a born storyteller, but also because, since she lived to be 100, we heard many of them again and again as a turn in a conversation would remind her of the time she stole hot loaves of bread from her aunt's windowsill, tried to poison her grammar school teacher with chalk, or wrung the neck of a fighting rooster who lost his fight and thus her wager.

Toward the end of her life, Oma began typing up her life story and later dictating other portions to my mother, her only daughter. Under the surface of the stories runs a common theme of how the spirited "little rooster," while perhaps never quite as beautiful or good as her blond and obedient older sister Vera, stirred up peaceful life wherever she went.

Haantje was born on November 23, 1896 in Curaçao, Netherlands Antilles, to a Swedish cabin boy become sea captain, Johannes Johansson, and his much younger Dutch wife, Jacomina Maria Catherina van Eps. Her years in Curaçao were probably the happiest of her life so it was not surprising that, in her final days, her mind returned to Curaçao and her parents.

One of her favorite stories from those years concerned a trip she and Vera took on one of her father's sister ships to visit La Guayra, Venezuela, to celebrate carnival.

***

Carnival was exciting but we were scared, too; so many people dancing around and spraying us with perfume... The youngest of the family [we were visiting], Johan, about three years older than me, had a crush on me. He came on horseback one night to serenade me, and the other girls had to push me out of bed to go to the window and accept the rose he threw into the room. After he finished the song, he played the guitar too. I told him: "Johan, I am sleepy. Why don't you go home?" Home was a two-hour ride back to town. That was the romantic streak in me! But it did not cool him off, he wrote me letters for years and I took them to my Spanish class. The teachers and other students enjoyed them.

***

Haantje's life took her from Curaçao to Holland, Sumatra, Java, Banda Aceh, New York City, and eventually Hartford, Connecticut. Along the way she bore and raised three children; skied the Swiss Alps; saw Josephine Baker dance in a nightclub in Paris; attended the 1936 Olympic Games in Germany and saw Goebbels in the stands; watched Winston Churchill review her husband's troops in Nijmegen; fled Indonesia just months before the Japanese invasion; sailed through Pearl Harbor the week before the infamous attack; began a new life as a working woman at the Dutch embassy in New York City; attended the christening party for the exiled Dutch princesses in Canada; reunited with a son who survived a Nazi concentration camp; worked as a bookkeeper at Traveler's Insurance Company in Hartford; and retired at age sixty-five. She took enormous satisfaction from the fact that her longevity earned her thirty-five years of pension checks and raises (as she called her cost of living increases).

Her stories often noted only in passing the incidents of crossing paths with some of the world's most famous people. Instead she would focus on the small human interactions and off-color or embarrassing moments that would bring roars of laughter when her Curaçao crowd got together to swap memories.

Haantje with koala bears in Australia circa 1945.

***

One day [in Nijmegen, The Netherlands] there was a special ceremony to unveil the statue of a public official. When they pulled away the veil, everyone was surprised to see a chamber pot under the bishop's seat. The culprits of this deed were never found.

***

Haantje was a well-read person, always deeply interested in world events, yet neither her verbal anecdotes nor her written memoirs give any mention of issues such as the controversy over the morality of supporting Olympic games hosted by the Nazi regime. Of course, at the time, even the president of the international Olympic Association, after a short, closely managed inspection of German Olympic preparations, called for the 1936 games to go on, as he was satisfied that Jewish athletes were being treated fairly. Although Haantje's daughter Elly remembers that when they went to Austria "you could hear propaganda all the time about Hitler," Haantje's memoirs do not include the looming concerns she and her officer husband must have often discussed out of the children's hearing. Writing in her nineties, she appears to have confounded skiing trips to Austria with her memories of attending the Winter Olympics in Bavaria, Germany in 1936.

***

In 1926 my husband and I went to Vienna for the Winter Olympics. [There were no Olympics in Vienna, but she did go to Austria that year.] *Coming from Curaçao, I had never seen skiing nor ski jumping so it was quite a treat. We attended a concert in the open near the Danube River and there was plenty beer to be had, so I had trouble to get a soft drink. The orchestra was conducted by Richard Strauss (son of Johan Strauss) and it was touching when they played the Blue Danube while you could watch the Danube River. We attended the famous opera house in Vienna and I put on my best gown, but the Austrians were very poor and didn't dress for any occasion. The waiter at the coffee house, knowing we were strangers, complained people would come for a cup of coffee in order to get the daily paper to read and save the money to buy it. In later years we saw the performance of the famous Lipizzaner horses, which was incredible. In 1934* [The Winter Games were in 1936], *we went to the Winter Olympics in Lech (Austria).* [The Games were in Garmisch-Partenkirchen, Bavaria and her photo album shows pictures of her being there and of the Olympic stands. The family vacationed in Lech the following year.] *The #2 man of Germany, Goebbels, was there.*

***

Similarly, Haantje's stories never mention her emotions during the five years she lost contact with her oldest son and other Dutch relatives during the Nazi occupation of Holland (1940-1945). Instead, her memoir focuses on her work in New York City and several treasured social events where she was invited to join the royal Dutch family during the crown princess's exile in Canada. Haantje's husband had been a Lieutenant Colonel with the Dutch colonial forces in Indonesia when Holland was invaded in May of 1940. He and six other senior officers were called back to England by the Dutch Queen Wilhelmina, now in exile in London, to train any Dutch forces who had escaped from the Netherlands and were eager to fight to take back the Dutch colony of Indonesia. Against the wishes of the queen, the Dutch troops and officers prevailed and returned to the Pacific where, after years of training and planning, they eventually participated in the Allied liberation of Indonesia. Meanwhile, Haantje had attempted to travel to England to join her husband but Nazi attacks on Allied shipping made that trip impossible. She had to make hasty alternative plans that eventually brought her and her two youngest children to the U.S. Here, for the first time in her life, she had to work for a living and do all the household chores previously done by servants.

***

During WWII, jobs were plentiful in New York so I dropped them as if they were entertainment. Knowing three languages, stenography, typing, and bookkeeping – a knock at the door and I was in. Working for the Dutch consul in New York was very interesting but disappointing too. For example: a Dutch black sailor from Curaçao slapped a white officer in the face. After a hearing in New York, I went to translate the interview in a mental hospital. I was led in by two police officers and felt very sad when I saw so many sick people floating around in long, white garments although they seem happy because they were waltzing. The sailor was brought in between two policemen. As soon as he heard me speak Papiamento [the Creole language of Curaçao], *he went to town with his story He had been the only black sailor on the ship and, being religious, he read his Bible every day. When one officer took the Bible and threw it overboard, he got really mad and slapped him in the face. Returning to the office, I right away typed up the report and put it on the consul's desk for prompt action. He was not interested and I was very disappointed and could not understand his feelings, so ... I quit ... again.*

***

Born in a later time, Haantje's energy and intelligence would have brought her to a top leadership position in business or government. She was charismatic, ambitious, iron-willed, and strong; yet she had to content herself with the perks and privileges of her husband's career and the accomplishments of her children and grandchildren. However, those are the concerns of a granddaughter, not the grandmother herself. She knew she had lived an extraordinary life and took great delight in sharing her ultimate accomplishment – her stories. She would have been so pleased that they live on not only in her family's memories, but also in this book about growing up with the influence of magnificent women.

Elizabeth Vozzola

Inspiration

It wasn't until I became a mother that I realized the true dedication and love that my mother felt for me and my brother. If a child could realize this at a much younger age, then maybe the discovery of it during adulthood wouldn't be so life-changing. It seemed finally, at age thirty-three, that I realized that all the things my mother did, said, didn't do, etc. made sense. For example, when I was just ten years old, she protected me from one of the hardest lessons in life: death. Popeye, our Pekinese dog, was on the verge of dying. I didn't want to go to school. I just wanted to be there with everyone else even though I didn't understand what would inevitably happen. But you see, my mother knew. She knew that the outcome was going to be extremely painful for all of us. So, she told me I must go to school and that I wouldn't miss anything. It wasn't until about ten years later that I felt that pain, being with our second family dog as his life ended.

My mother didn't have an easy life in adulthood. She became a single mom when I was ten and my brother was twelve. She had to step into the working world after not working for twelve years and endure the many challenges that my brother's car accident left. Despite the many medical challenges she endured with my brother, she found time to improve herself for the betterment of her children. In between doctor's appointments, visits to physical therapy, and painful experiences with her son at rehabilitation centers, she knew that she had to further educate herself to be able to persevere in a dog-eat-dog world dominated by men in the workforce. I remember her dedication, even after a long hard day of working, doing homework with me, taking me to gymnastics, doctors' appointments for my brother, and so on, she would sit in her room and study for her real estate exam. She somehow focused her attention on me by including me and making me feel needed. I loved to reverse role play with her and be the one quizzing her on her studies as she often did for me. The outcome, of course, was that she passed her real estate exam and went on to be in the "Million Dollar Circle" year after year. Whether she knew it or not, those nights studying with her taught me that putting forth the effort in anything that you desire in life will lead to wonderful rewards.

These years for her must have been frightening, discouraging, and stressful yet she seemed to make it look so easy. I very rarely saw her cry and never saw her feel sorry for herself. She didn't turn to alcohol or drugs or become mentally depressed. Instead, she rose to the occasion with strength and courage. It turned out that she not only supported our family, but continued to be an outstanding professional in her career. Again, it is not until now that I realize her true strength. You see, for the last eighteen months I've been a "single mom" with three kids because of my husband's deployment with the Army. Her model of strength became an inspiration through this time in my life. Every time (and there were many) I wanted to just give up, I remembered all that my mother went through. She taught me to be a fighter and not to let life get me down.

Suzanne and her mother Antoinette.

My mother has molded and shaped my life and the person I have become. I've learned to laugh in the presence of chaos. I've learned to cry quietly inside, but always smile for my children. I've learned to seek out opportunities when dead ends seem to approach quickly. But most importantly, I've learned to embrace my mother and never forget the life lessons she taught me through her actions. I am forever indebted to her and only hope that I will be that kind of inspiration for my own daughters. My mother is Antoinette Jean (Puccio) Sica, the most inspirational woman I will ever know.

Suzanne (Sica) Bokenko

A Mother's Heart

My mother Kwi Boon Choi was born in Korea in 1901. Education was not common for every person at this time and was very expensive. She finished school only up to sixth grade. After my parents married, they moved to Japan for my father's mining business and lived there for twenty-five years. This was during the Japanese occupation of Korea which lasted from 1910 to 1945. My brothers, sisters, and I were born in Japan and originally had Japanese passports.

I remember my mother well. She never sat down and she never complained. She worked very, very hard all the time. She raised six children: my oldest brother, my three noisy sisters, and then me and my youngest brother. My father was busy managing a coal-mining company, but he sometimes had the chance to socialize with other men. My mother never had fun or time to herself. Her life was filled with work.

My father employed two or three dozen Korean men in the mine. They would come to our house at the end of a work day, their faces black with coal dust, to have dinner at our house before they went home. My mother cooked every day for all these people in addition to us. She would be in the kitchen for many hours preparing whatever food she could get, maybe fish or soup or rice, and they would come in after work and eat. I remember being in the kitchen with her, watching her work without stopping all day long.

In 1946, one year after WWII ended, we moved back to Korea. Four years later the Korean War started. During the Korean War, everyone who disliked communism moved south, and many people were living in the streets in the winter. It was very difficult to survive during those years. My father and mother allowed people to come into our house and stay with us without paying rent. About ten families lived all together in our house. My mother took care of everybody and shared everything we had.

My oldest brother, who was ten years older than I, joined the army and was killed within one year. Now I, as the oldest son, was responsible for the family. I was still young and quite weak and thin, but I tried my best to grow up quickly so I could take care of everyone.

Even after the Korean War the family had a very difficult time. To earn a little money, my mother had a small private boarding house for students in our home. I rushed to finish my education at Seoul National University so I could get a job and bring everybody to Seoul.

When I got a job after graduating from the University in 1963, it was her time to relax. I was the oldest son and I was determined to make her life easy by taking care of her and providing for her. I rented, and later bought, a house in Seoul where we all lived together very happily.

By 1970 I had achieved many things in my profession including teaching at the University, designing interiors for the "White House" of Korea, and being appointed by the mayor of Seoul as his official design consultant. There was no additional career advancement possible for me unless we moved. By this time, also, I was married and had two children. My father encouraged us to leave Korea. We considered our options and chose to move to Canada.

I have felt very guilty that we left Korea instead of staying to help make my mother's life easier. My wife and I encouraged my parents to come to Canada and live with us. They came for a visit, but it was too difficult for them to make the adjustment to all the differences in culture and language.

My mother's life was all about hard work. She was very poor, but she never moaned and grumbled. She never had a chance to think about herself or make choices in her own life. All of her time was occupied with children, my father, and the miners or others living and eating with us. She was never out of the house and never finished with her work. She lived through two wars and never had carefree times or fun. Even when she was dying at eighty-eight years old, she did not complain. She would say, "I'm okay! Don't worry about me!"

My father was famous for his beautiful calligraphy and I may have inherited my artistic sensibility from him, but my heart comes from my mom and is filled with all that I owe her. She had to be strong-minded to survive the hardships of her life without bitterness, but she also had a soft and loving heart that embraced and sustained her family and many others.

Hyo Kim

Great Aunt Plenty and Great Aunt Peace

Rose really did have some cause to be sad; for she had no mother, and had lately lost her father also, which left her no home but this with her great-aunts. She had been with them only a week, and, though the dear old ladies had tried their best to make her happy, they had not succeeded very well, for she was unlike any child they had ever seen, and they felt very much as if they had the care of a low-spirited butterfly.

They had given her the freedom of the house, and for a day or two she had amused herself roaming all over it, for it was a capital old mansion, and was full of all manner of odd nooks, charming rooms, and mysterious passages. Windows broke out in unexpected places, little balconies overhung the garden most romantically, and there was a long upper hall full of curiosities from all parts of the world; for the Campbells had been sea-captains for generations.

Aunt Plenty had even allowed Rose to rummage in her great china closet, – a spicy retreat, rich in all the "goodies" that children love; but Rose seemed to care little for these toothsome temptations; and when that hope failed, Aunt Plenty gave up in despair.

Gentle Aunt Peace had tried all sorts of pretty needle-work, and planned a doll's wardrobe that would have won the heart of even an older child. But Rose took little interest in pink satin hats and tiny hose, though she sewed dutifully till her aunt caught her wiping tears away with the train of a wedding-dress, and that discovery put an end to the sewing society.

Then both old ladies put their heads together and picked out the model child of the neighborhood to come and play with their niece. But Ariadne Blish was the worst failure of all, for Rose could not bear the sight of her, and said she was so like a wax doll she longed to give her a pinch and see if she would squeak. So prim little Ariadne was sent home, and the exhausted aunties left Rose to her own devices for a day or two.

Bad weather and a cold kept her in-doors, and she spent most of her time in the library where her father's books were stored. Here she read a great deal, cried a little, and dreamed many of the innocent bright dreams in which imaginative children find such comfort and delight. This suited her better than any thing else, but it was not good for her, and she grew pale, heavy-eyed, and listless, though Aunt Plenty gave her iron enough to make a cooking-stove, and Aunt Peace petted her like a poodle.

Seeing this, the poor aunties racked their brains for a new amusement, and determined to venture a bold stroke, though not very hopeful of its success. They said nothing to Rose about their plan for this Saturday afternoon, but let her alone till the time came for the grand surprise, little dreaming that the odd child would find pleasure for herself in a most unexpected quarter.

Louisa M. Alcott

Bunia

I have always wished my grandmother to be like the grandmother of my friend Maria: living in a little house in a small town, tending to an enormous garden and sending the fruits of her labor to Maria and her parents. Judging by the amount of red currents and gooseberries I saw spilling from buckets and baskets in Maria's kitchen, I assumed the garden was huge. Maria was my best friend and sometimes I went with her to visit her grandma, and I played with Maria's cousins in that beautiful garden (which turned out to be rather modest in size).

I lived in an old downtown apartment, in an old, secession nineteenth-century building, which, like an old woman, retained some beautiful features but could not hide the toll of passing years. There was no yard to play in, and the staircase leading to our apartment was damp, smelly, dark, and very frightening. The closest park was at least ten minutes away and I could only dream about seeing trees through the windows. Instead I could see other old buildings, street cars, and hurried passersby.

My mother's mother was the only grandparent I ever knew; all the others died before I was born. Both my grandfathers perished in wars; one died while fighting in the Polish-Russian war of 1920; the other was murdered by Nazis. My dad's mother died of cancer.

My grandmother did not live in a small town in a cozy house surrounded by a prolific garden. She lived with us, sharing a room with my sister and me. The room was divided by a sophisticated labyrinth of bookcases and wardrobes to create three separate dens. My parents occupied another room that during the day served as a living room, dining room, and also as a study where they would discuss especially difficult medical cases. They were both oncologists.

The kitchen in our apartment wasn't big; it was rather dark, mostly because its only window (facing north) was awkwardly positioned in the corner. The other window, along with the other half of the kitchen, belonged to our neighbors. Our government had declared that the original four-room apartment was too big for one family and divided it into two separate, two-room units. Each time we entered the apartment after a vacation, our kitchen looked even darker than before. But this was the place where my grandmother spent most of her time. There she sat and read books and newspapers. There she cooked, and there I learned about Poland's difficult past. Before I took an official history course in elementary school I was already "indoctrinated" by my grandmother. It was she who told me about Stalin attacking Poland from the east two weeks after Hitler invaded it from the west. The "official", school-taught version stated that Stalin and his soldiers marched into Poland to help us fend off Germans. It was she who told me about Katyn, the place where Russians murdered thousands of Polish officers, a fact so conveniently absent in my public schooling.

My grandmother wasn't a warm, loving granny; she wasn't a fashionable professional woman. She did not have many friends. Nevertheless, she was a modern, brave, and independent woman. She was born in 1885 as the youngest of twelve siblings; all of whom, except for one brother, died at a young age. Her family's land and residence were confiscated as punishment for their involvement in one of the major Polish uprisings against Russia in 1863, and her grandfather was sent to Siberia for thirty years.

My grandmother was well educated and started working in her late teens as a teacher in high schools for girls. Before and during the big Russian revolution (and WWI) she was a tutor of Polish language and history in the underground education system. She also earned money by embroidering banners for the Polish army and churches. She continued to work even after marrying my grandfather and bringing up three children.

She never told me about the adventures of her life. Only later, I learned from my aunt about Grandma's escape with three little children from Minsk in Belarus (then part of Poland), taking "the last train" before the Red Revolution's army flooded it. During that time, my grandfather fought on the WWI fronts. I guess that what I see as major historical events were, for her, just life and not too interesting to talk about.

For her whole life she was a true Polish patriot and did not yield under communistic Russian occupation or the Nazi's domination during WWII. To survive through these calamitous times, a strong presence of mind and also discretion were keys to survival. Maybe that is why she did not talk much about herself, even afterwards.

I remember sitting on a little stool behind the door, listening to my grandmother boss around our housekeeper, a woman who was with my family for as long as I remember. She was coming to help with cleaning and shopping and was always defending me against any critique I was getting from my mom and grandma. My grandma and she were not the best of friends; they had some tough moments together, yet I think they were fond of each other. I did not pay too much attention to their conversations; I was waiting eagerly to be allowed to help. It rarely happened since my grandmother did not have patience to sit and wait until I managed to separate egg yolk from egg white or skin from almonds. She liked to cook, frequently trying to recreate dishes from her childhood, despite the frugality and limits of communistic commerce in Poland. Our kitchen was filled with the sweet smell of prune preserves and loganberry jam, the sweets I tried to make later in my adult life. My grandma loved mushrooms and there was an unlimited supply of those dry, wrinkled morsels which she used in almost every dish.

She treated me and my friends as adults, and I remember celebrating her name day with her when Maria and I were about thirteen. It was just the three of us. She baked a special cake and we toasted her with real eggnog, her favorite drink, next to cognac. In these instances, some of her fearlessness prevailed, and she never hesitated to tell Maria that she hated communism. She encouraged us to get involved in the underground movement, knowing full well that Maria's father was a high-ranking party member and that those bold statements could have serious consequences. She never asked questions or pried into our lives and never offered us advice. Still, I always tried to guess what she would approve of and to please her.

I remember my grandmother as a tired, plump old lady with a dry sense of humor reading or cooking in the dark kitchen. In her other incarnation she was also a brave woman surviving the most adverse situations and protecting her children, a woman who was a fierce supporter of independence and freedom of her country, and a professional working woman at the very beginning of the twentieth century. I love her in both her incarnations and I hope I have a little of both in me; love of food and cooking and fondness for lilies-of-the-valley, as well as her rebellious streak and curiosity toward new events and people. Regardless of the interesting things I have learned about her difficult life, what I feel most deeply when I think about my grandma is the warmth and love coming from the aroma of food and her laughter.

Elzbieta Sikora

Bunia is a loving term for grandmother. In Polish, grandmother is babcia; Grammy would be babunia, and my way of calling her was just bunia. It is pronounced "boonya."

SECTION FIVE

Threads and Themes and Ties that Bind Us

Mama was no longer afraid. Her face glowed with peace and happiness. We traded confidences, compassion, and love – all those things that only a mother and daughter can share.

For so long I'd wished to be part of a sisterhood. I hadn't found it in the women's chambers with my cousins when I was alive, because they hadn't liked me ... But I had it with my mother and grandmother. Despite our weaknesses and failings, a single thread bound us together: my grandmother, as confused as she was; my mother, as broken as she was; and me, a pathetic hungry ghost. As Mama and I walked on through the night, I understood that I was not alone.

Lisa See
Peony in Love

Kimono Threads

All of the women in my family create beautiful things. My mom loves to sew clothes for me and my sister as a hobby, and her mother liked to crochet. This story is about my father's mother who had a beautiful hobby – she would make traditional Japanese kimono.

One time my grandmother's neighbor asked her to make kimono for her children. I saw her sewing at her dining room table when I went to visit her in the summer. My grandmother was sewing kimono for other kids and I was very jealous. I was about eight or ten years old and I remember thinking that the kimono she was making would not fit me. This scene stayed in my mind for a long time.

Years later, when I was graduating from college, I decided to wear a traditional kimono of the style from eighty to one hundred years ago. This style of kimono and hakama was like a uniform at that time for girls in school. It was very traditional to wear this style for graduation.

My mom and I went to the kimono shop and selected the silk piece goods and then my grandmother sewed a beautiful and precious kimono for me.

The graduation day was very busy. I had to go to the hair salon at 7:00 a.m. and then come home and get dressed. My mother helped me get dressed. I was very nervous. We had to be at the ceremony by 11:00 a.m.

I kept saying to my mom, "Hurry up! Hurry up!" I couldn't stand still even though I was wearing the kimono. I was running here and there in our house.

While I was rushing around, a door knob caught my kimono sleeve. I didn't realize it was stuck, and I pulled hard. The kimono sleeve ripped! This was horrible! My mind was blank;

Mizuho wearing her graduation kimono.

I couldn't think of what to do. I was surprised ... I was afraid ... I was thinking I could not go to the graduation ceremony.

We have a saying in Japanese, *Seite ha koto wo shisonnjiru* that means *Haste makes waste.*

My mother was getting ready herself, but she stopped and looked at my sleeve. She was very quiet. She came to me with her needle and thread and she began to fix the ripped sleeve. The time when she was sewing may have been short, possibly only three or four minutes, but it was an eternity for me. That time seemed magical. I didn't watch her sew. I couldn't see where the sleeve was ripped and, when she was finished, I couldn't see where she had fixed it.

My mom and I went to the graduation ceremony together, and it surprised me to learn that we were on time.

Now in my kimono there are two threads: one my grandmom used to make the kimono and one my mom used to fix it. It is precious to me for all the meanings of tradition, celebration, and the skills of women in my family whose love became visible in my beautiful kimono.

Mizuho Kawasaki

A Stitch of Time

Every night as I crawl into bed, I slip under a quilt made of a patchwork of purple-themed fabrics. There are dark indigo purples, light lavender purples, and every kind of purple that exists betwixt the two. There are purple flowers, purple stripes, and even purple solids. This quilt is nearly fourteen years old now, and I have quite outgrown my purple phase, but it is still one of my most prized possessions. There is a far more beautiful and varied quilt on my couch at home, with thirty-six kimonos as its blocks, every one of which I made over three unbearably dull snow days when I was fourteen. And there are the two quilts in a home in Cambridge, one on the bed of my parents' dearest friends, and the other on the bed of my own best friend. The former is the first quilt my mother and I ever made together, constructed a few months before my own purple concoction. This quilt is a gorgeous piece made up of red, black, and white Asian-themed fabrics: A bold beginner's piece that has since been repaired many times.

The quilt adorning my friend's bed was my first time going it alone. I broke away from the log cabin set-up with which my mother and I were so comfortable, and simply spent one afternoon cutting out 150 five-inch squares out of six batik fabrics and laying them out in a pattern on the floor. The fabrics I chose were colorful, soft, and extremely tropical. As I shuffled them around on the floor for hours, a pattern slowly emerged: sand yellows, sunset oranges, and hyacinth pinks in the middle, with kiwi greens and tropical ocean blues radiating outwards toward the blue color of the ocean depths and the indigo purple of the night sky. I sewed a fabric copy of a photo of myself and my friend from when we were about eight years old and a stitched message of friendship onto the quilt's back, "To Molly, My Best Friend, I Love You." I gave it to her as a sixteenth birthday present, and my mother still thinks it's the most beautiful quilt to come out of our house.

And yet it is still my purple quilt – rough, messy, and out-of-date – which I cannot bear to be without. In the fanciest hotels, under the softest of blankets, I find myself missing my familiar cotton contraption. This is the quilt which has absorbed late-night tears as well as giggles, secrets as well as promises: the perfect confidant. This is the quilt which I wrapped around myself as I walked through my house the night my grandmother died, while everyone else slept and I was awake thinking. This is the quilt that reminds me of being eight years old, cutting carefully along an edge and ironing a seam while my mother gave directions from her seat at the sewing machine. This is the quilt whose straight lines and frayed edges I have memorized through wakeful nights, tracing the angles and seams as my mind refused to quiet. This is my nightly reminder that life can be simple and, through that simplicity, good. No matter what the daylight may display when I venture out from the safety of my second night-skin; no matter what quarrels, concerns, deadlines, or obligations are thrown at me under the bright sun; I know that when the light fades, I can crawl under a layer of simple goodness.

When I packed up for my freshman year of college, I kept the quilt rolled up next to me in the backseat of my mother's car as my family drove to New York. And when two months later, I tore through the delicate, top layer of the quilt, I was struck dumb and stone-still before racing for the phone. I smoothed over the tear with my hand while waiting for my mother to pick up; when she did, I blurted out what I had done, in the sad, guilty tones of a child who's broken a pretty something, in their minds irreparably. My mother, busy in her office, simply said, "Well, fix it, then." And so I did. I took out the small sewing kit my mother had bought in a drugstore the day I moved into my dorm, and searched through the threads for one that most closely matched my faded quilt. The purples were no longer quite so vibrant, and the tear rent the palest part, so that the most suitable thread was an off-white, slightly tan color. I sat on my college-issued, narrow, extra-long mattress in New York, and carefully stitched up the tear, focused as much on my memories as on the work in my hands – after all, the memories of my mother were my guide to how to repair quilts, along with pretty much everything else.

Once I'd doubled back over the final few stitches a final few times, hoping to prevent a future tear, I snipped the thread and regarded my handiwork. It was not as precise as what my mother or I could do with a machine, nor as neat as what she could do by hand, but that I could do it at all was a testament to her, and to me. Tracing the stitches, I thought about the day when I would tuck my own little girl in under this quilt, and show her the rip her mummy had sewn up. And I hoped I'd do well enough by my daughter that she'd have a quilt of her own to one day rip and repair, all on her own.

Liz Maroney

Resemblance

I must have been five or six when I first heard it. "You look just like your mother." Often this remark came from strangers, from cashiers or waitresses. I was indifferent; however, I'd notice that my mom smiled.

As I grew older and the comments were more frequent, I became annoyed. "I'm ten years old," I thought, "and I look nothing like a woman twenty-four years my senior." I could acknowledge that we shared the same eyes, dark hair, freckles, and strong posture, but I wanted to look like me, not someone else. I was a kid; I didn't want to look like an adult.

In my teens, it became even more common. How on earth could I look like my mom when I was so damn cool, and she was a mom with three kids? She didn't have feathered hair or wear Calvin Klein's or adore Cyndi Lauper. It was amusingly irritating.

At the age of thirty-three, I joined an extended family dinner in honor of my late grandmother in Akron, Ohio. Walking into the restaurant alone I heard excited voices from across the restaurant. "There's Sally!" Only it wasn't Sally; it was me, Laura.

As I met relatives and old family friends, their mistake was suddenly charming. I did look like her, and it was a hell of a compliment. I could only hope to look as beautiful and strong as my mom.

Now, on my bedroom bureau, there is a photo of her in her mid-twenties. Even my husband thinks that it's me ... but it's her, and I'll treasure our resemblance forever.

Laura de Kreij

Cossacks

One day when I was a teenager, my mother and I were sitting at the kitchen table talking. Suddenly, she said: "Nancy, notice how you're sitting."

I was on the very edge of my chair, with my feet flat on the floor. I thought my mom was criticizing, but when I started to shift my position, she shook her head.

"Look at me," she said. "I'm sitting the same way you are." She nodded wisely. "My mother sat this way, too. And her mother before her." She leaned forward. "Do you know why?"

I shook my head.

"Cossacks," said my mother, as we sat in a ranch house in suburban Peabody, Massachusetts. "You've got to be ready to run."

Nancy Werlin

Family Rings

In life, my grandmothers gave me experiences that helped shape my spirit and beliefs. In death, they gave me the rings off their fingers.

My grandmothers were next-door neighbors for many years. I love to tell friends about how my mother married the boy next door. And I revel in the stories that my parents have told about sledding together in their adjoining back yards with their younger siblings.

As a result of their differing heritages and traditions, what I learned from each of them is unique. If I could cuddle within the circle of their grandmotherly arms today, as I did as a child, here's what I'd tell them …

Grandma Carubia, I remember going to church with you on Sunday mornings followed by traditional, multi-course Italian meals. The sweet aroma of homemade tomato sauce permeated your home. On holidays, your kitchen table stretched into the living room as far as my eyes could see. You always set a table for the younger grandkids covered with a festive table cloth, just like the grown-up table. You reserved a seat for me in the kitchen: the one with the orange and green cushion to your left, against the window, next to the refrigerator – the best seat because it was next to you. You were a gracious host with a natural ability to make everyone feel at home. The sounds and smells of a house full of friends and family remind me of you. Although you sometimes surprised me with small gifts that you knew I would adore (especially trinkets from the Avon catalog), you placed a greater emphasis on experiences. Even though I was one of many grandchildren, you always made me feel special.

Grandma Glorie, you taught me to appreciate the finer things in life. Some of my early memories of time spent together are picnics; boat cruises on the Hudson River; and lazy afternoons in your yard. When I was a little older and expressed an interest in antiques, you taught me about "junkin" – finding treasures in other people's junk. One of my cherished belongings is a wing-back chair that I found on trash day. I reupholstered the chair with a rich, ruby-red fabric with a diamond, gold-leaf pattern. When you were in your late seventies, you were hospitalized with a respiratory illness. I made a wholehearted attempt to motivate you to hang on to life by saying, "Grandma, would you please make a baby quilt for some day when I start a family?" In your typical, matter-of-fact style, you responded, "I already made baby quilts for you and your brother to give to your children when that day comes. They're in the cedar chest upstairs in my house." You were an incredibly thoughtful, patient, and resourceful woman.

Of Grandma Carubia's twelve grandchildren, I am the oldest girl. When she died, I inherited her timeless, square-set, diamond engagement ring and wedding band. The platinum bands had worn down with time – evidence of a long, enduring marriage. A year after she passed away, my husband-to-be proposed marriage by "surprising" me with her engagement ring. I married him the following year on a stunningly beautiful autumn day. I was so proud to wear the rings that Grandma had worn for more than fifty years.

Grandma Glorie passed away soon after the terrorist attacks on the World Trade Towers in New York City. I remember the air seeming fresh and crisp at the cemetery on the day we buried her ashes, after having spent weeks inhaling remnants of the Trade Towers while living and working in my Manhattan apartment. When she died, I inherited her family ring of three gemstones; the birthstones of her children.

Today, the rings sit side-by-side in my jewelry box. The diamond rings sit untouched. Even though my marriage disintegrated, I keep the rings in view. They remind me not of my failed relationship, but of the love that my grandparents shared. The gemstone ring serves as a daily reminder of the importance of family.

I take comfort in catching daily glimpses of the jewels that once adorned my grandmothers' hands. Their grandmotherly energy reunites each day to surround me with the unchanging brilliance of their love, support, and wisdom. I'll be sure to pass along some of my grandmothers' lessons to my two sons. We're off to a great start! They love when we entertain guests, and one of their favorite meals is spaghetti with homemade meatballs made using Grandma Carubia's recipe. They adore picnics, and both slip into sweet dreams each night under the comfort of Grandma Glorie's quilts.

Michele Glorie Palmer

Stride Piano

My mother was one of twelve children who grew up quite poor in St. Mary's, Pennsylvania. My grandmother's dying words were, "Don't fight over my money!" The joke was that there was no money whatsoever. My grandfather was a tailor and he would barter for whatever goods and services they needed as a family. He would even barter with the dentist. There was no exchange of money. By today's standards, they were poor.

As a child, my mother taught herself how to play the piano "by ear." She had a musical gift of the ability to hear a tune and then somehow learn to play it. She developed her gift by going to church and watching the organist. There were foot pedals on the church organ, and she watched the motion of the organist's feet moving back and forth from left to right. She began playing the piano by imitating with her left hand that motion of the organist's foot. She was playing chords and a rhythm with her left hand, and eventually, she picked up the skill of playing the melody with her right hand.

Peg Herbst Vollmer, June 1944, at Knotty Pine Camp.

This style of playing was called stride piano. Fats Waller was a famous stride musician in the 1920s. Stride piano is a form of jazz and it's rather happy music.

My mother played a lot on the black keys of the piano keyboard, the sharps and flats. This was very difficult, but that's what came naturally to her. Her brothers each played a different musical instrument – saxophone, cello, trumpet, violin – and they would adjust their playing to her key.

When she was growing up, all the children had chores to do, washing the dishes, cleaning, and all that, but she never had to do chores. Her brothers and sisters would say, "Marg, you play the piano and we'll do the chores! Chores are easier and faster when you are playing the piano."

Mom always felt self conscious about her playing because she didn't have formal training or lessons of any kind. She didn't think that she was very good.

Music was something I heard all the time when I was growing up. In the background of many of my childhood memories, Mom is playing the piano. Sometimes we would all sing along. We enjoyed it, certainly, but I think that mostly, we just took it for granted. The more I think about it now, the more I realize how remarkable she was. Her piano playing was the theme music of a happy family for at least two generations.

Alice Clark

Warp & Weft

Cotton, wool, and silk
Come alive in your hands
You have wrapped those you love
In color, in beauty.

Full skirted olive green
A paisley bodice laced in red
I was Maid Marion
In my Robin Hood dress.

Flour speckled black jersey
Thundering down a dirt road
I was the wronged child watching you
Chase my tormenter to ground.

White satin and Alencon lace
Two hundred hours of careful love
Most thought I was a hurried bride
You knew the wait was over.

Silver lamé for maternity
A walking Christmas ornament
I was a pregnant disco ball
Dancing like a dervish, near full term.

The white satin and Alencon lace
Reappearing in a baby's bonnet once, twice
Mingled with inherited blue satin
A fourth generation in bespoke christening.

All these years of love I could touch
Anytime I needed it
Strong and soft, warp and weft
Foundation for everything good.

Joyce O'Donnell Maroney

Hairloom

Gold and silver, white
and auburn strands still
thread the eyes after years
inside this round tin of
bobby-pins, pool of linked
wires my grandmother kept long
after she had any use for them.

A single mother divorced
at thirty, she'd suffer
all night with a head baited
for love – pin curls wrapped
in a babushka – dreaming
of a husband, one who'd stick
this time. Or maybe hoping

the metal rods would hold
her, somehow, together.
A husband never came
despite her efforts, though
every now and then the silken
art the crude clips made of her
hair would mesmerize a man.

But the pins had other plans
to hold her sister's blond curls
tightly to her scalp, her daughters'
braids in landscaped rows
along the hairline, fractured
neatly by a heavy part
centered from front to back.

As children, my sister and I
endured the pronged things
to snag our long locks
in a twisted bun like a crown.
We never doubted the power
of the pins to keep us lovely
through hours of dance recitals.

Simple tin of coiffure aids,
I know the magic you hold.
My mother keeps you in a drawer

she sometimes opens to remove
your lid, generations of fragrance
waft and untangle her memory,
our perfumes mixed as one.

Rebecca Clever

Daughters of Ann

While working on a genealogy project for our family, my late brother Raymond made a fascinating discovery: every mother going back over 200 years had the name Ann in one form or another. I am Anna Marie Nachman; my mother was Anna Barbara Kendrick; her mother was Anna Veronica Roskovensky; hers was Anna Klein; and hers was Anna Hudak; and the furthest back he went he found Susanna Zahornavszky. My daughter AnneLiese and I sing together and my brother's discovery made it easy for me to come up with a name for our musical group – we are, Daughters of Ann!

My mother worked outside the home to help my father support their six children. I, the youngest, stayed with my grandmother while my mother and father worked. By this time in her life, Grandma lived alone. All of her children were grown. My grandfather had been killed in a mining accident when my mother was sixteen years old. I wish I had known him. My grandmother was left to raise her six children alone. She suffered other tragedies in her life prior to my grandfather's death. She also lost three children; two sons to illness and a daughter who was accidentally scalded to death when she was but six years old. Although she had many tragedies in her life, Grandma's faith was strong and I only recall her being happy and most often, smiling. I was nine years old when my grandmother died but I have very fond memories of her.

She was rather short and stout. Her gray hair was always neatly braided and wound into a bun at the back of her head. I remember her humming and rocking me to sleep on warm summer days on her front porch glider. She had a lovely flower garden on the front lawn in front of that porch and vegetables and herbs just outside the kitchen. It was in her kitchen where I remember spending the most time with her; where she could be found in her apron, busily preparing many delicious treats. Coming from the "old country" of Czechoslovakia, she brought with her many traditional recipes. Her daily life revolved around cooking, baking, canning, making wine, embroidering, crocheting, making rag rugs, farming, and praying. I get exhausted just thinking about all she must have done, but being a small child at the time, I only remember the goodies like sugar buns in a large tin canister in the closet under the steps, or canned pears, and red raspberry jam from the cellar. Even now, when I open a jar of raspberry jam and inhale that wonderful aroma, it takes me back to those days!

One recipe I inherited from my grandmother is a beef and vegetable soup with homemade noodles which my mother also made and my children dubbed "Grammy Soup." The soup itself is fairly simple to make; we use whole, peeled vegetables so there is no chopping. The noodles, however, are a skill to be mastered. My mother did it with lightning speed and precision. My noodles, however, are crafted slowly and no matter how careful I am, they vary in size from extra thin to extra wide!

Grandma and a very young Anna Marie.

In July 2007, I became a grandmother and made my first pot of "Grammy Soup" as an official Grammy. I proudly carry on the tradition as a daughter of Ann and hope my daughter will as well.

Anna Marie Nachman

Reel Time

I love movies, every single aspect of them, the whole experience from beginning to end. My maternal grandfather so loves movies that he carries around the movie times for his favorite cinema in the breast pocket of his polo shirt wherever he goes, in case he should have some free time during the day. His own father apparently loved movies from the first time he ever saw them, without sound or color. And of course, there's my mother, who loves movies as much as both of them, and nearly as much as I do.

When she was pregnant with me, my mother had a lot of free time on her hands, and even received three weeks extra free time, due to my late arrival. Though she'd always gone to see movies, during those last three weeks of pregnancy, she went to see movies every day. According to her reasoning, she should be surrounded by people in case something happened, and she also shouldn't overexert herself. What a perfect excuse to go to the movies! My mother saw "Moonstruck" at least three times during her last month of pregnancy. After I was born, however, she devoted herself to being a stay-at-home mom for three months before she went back to work.

When my brother was born two years later, the same happened again, though with fewer movies, as she now had to deal with a devilish toddler. When my brother was three months old, once again my mother re-entered the workforce. She started her career in the late seventies, and was of the generation determined to prove that women could work just as hard as their male counterparts. If romance, marriage, and children didn't slow men down, these women wouldn't allow those things to hinder them either. So my mother worked and continues to work long hours, every day, cementing a foundation for subsequent generations of working women. While admirable, this means my mother comes home from work late nearly every day, leaving little time for family bonding or even just chitchat about our days.

For every problem my mother has ever encountered, she has found a solution or, at the very least, some compensation, and this was no exception. Searching for a good way to spend time with her young daughter, my mother found her solution: the movies. My mom took me to the movies once or twice a month, just the two of us, though, in addition, we went to the movies as a family at least three times a month. Looking back, I realize that my dad must have recognized this as mother-daughter time, because he willingly stayed behind, convincing my brother Ted that a video and pizza would be better than whatever movie his mother and sister were seeing. For me, a dark theater with a hundred other people and questionable food was just perfect because I was with my mother.

Even though we wouldn't talk during the movie, during the previews we'd chatter about anything and everything. At the end of a good preview, my mom would turn to me with a certain look and say "We'll be seeing that." Every time she saw a good preview, she'd say the same thing: "We'll be seeing that." I loved the little ritual, groomed my tastes to hers, and gauged her reaction during a preview, so that I might be the one to say, "We'll be seeing that." Once the movie started, though, we wouldn't say anything. During scary movies, we'd grip each other's arms or squeal under our breath. She tended to turn to me when her arm snaked around my forearm, and no matter how frightened I was, when she turned to me, I couldn't help but smile, because this was all mine, and no one else's.

Movie buddies.

During comedies, when she'd throw her head back in laughter, I followed suit, to the point that there'd be two guffawing maniacs in the theater. Neither one of us cared that everyone might be staring. We wrapped ourselves in the magic blanket of anonymity. Clenching my mother's arm in feigned terror, throwing my laughter up to the roof or bending over double with it, I was close to my favorite movie buddy, my mother, my idol. Those dark theaters were my houses of worship, and returning to them now, even without her company, is my way of connecting with her, of claiming her as my own, even if only for a few hours.

Liz Maroney

Layer by Layer

With each layer of wallpaper that I removed from the nineteenth-century kitchen cupboard, a new design of color, flower, and charm was revealed. While I worked at peeling and scraping, my thoughts evolved from a mindless jumble to memories of my mother. It all started with the thought that the old wallpaper patterns were so exquisite and somewhat feminine. From there I just knew that it had to be women, most likely mothers, who had adorned this simple kitchen piece. I could sense the presence of those before me. I was doing with my hands what had been done over and over on this wood before. A transformation to a new richness and beauty was often due to a woman's special touch. I know that because it was my mother's way.

My mother had many "special touches" that I thought about while I worked on this "spirited" piece of furniture. I felt her love as a child by her actions. When a tooth fell out, there would be a demitasse cup to hold the treasured object until the tooth fairy picked it up (always on time, too). A made-to-order prom dress would be created with the requested bows and trim. My mother would hug and kiss me in such a way that I could truly feel how important I was to the world around me. She would go through catalogs with me hunting for the perfect bedspread and curtains to make my newly painted room complete. On Thursday afternoons she would have a "coffee clutch" with her female friends and bake special desserts to treat her friends and her family too!

It goes on and on. She would come alive with excitement when relatives planned a visit, and her anticipation would fill me and become my excitement too. When we had company, she prepared gourmet meals, reminisced in a more carefree way about the special family moments of her youth, and greatly contributed to an atmosphere of extended family bonding. I could tell that my cousins loved her because she would hug and kiss them in that special way. She had a special touch. All these warm thoughts about my mother flowed through my mind while I stripped away the layers of wallpaper.

Thoughts surfaced about her "special touches" into my adult years. She remembered special occasions, she spent time with me and my family, she cooked special meals for us with plenty of leftovers to bring home, she visited me, she cared for my children, and so much more. She was someone who would take the time to wallpaper the inside of a kitchen cupboard to add a special touch to the atmosphere in a home. She was the one who taught me how to be a mother.

My daughter Taryn, totally unaware of my mind's journey, came down to the cellar to see how this project of mine was going. Out of the blue, she asked me if she could keep this cupboard in her room. Immediately, I knew that this cupboard had a destiny to be in our home, and that Taryn was to be its next caretaker. Something was set in motion, and we were in the midst of an instinctual mother-child dance. In brief seconds I envisioned going with my daughter to pick out her wallpaper pattern of distinction and teaching her how to measure and paste. Through this piece of furniture, I could transmit my love and skill to my daughter while she created a "special touch" for her living space.

What started out as a dull task for me that Saturday morning was transformed into an emotional bowl of chicken soup. I recognized that the continuity and heritage of women helps me bear the grief I still feel from my mother's death. When my mind is open to it, my mother's special touch is close by. I feel her presence lingering among the layers of wallpaper.

Nina Snyder

Faccia Malute

A small cloth pouch, no bigger than my thumb, hangs in my dining room. The pouch is red with tiny white polka dots and is cinched with a strand of variegated yarn in green, white, and red – the colors of the Italian flag. In my family, we call this pouch a *faccia malute*, though none of us knows exactly what that means. A ward, a charm – it is a gift made by my mother that is supposed to protect me from malocchio, the evil eye. If you squeeze the pouch, it feels soft and a little crunchy. You can feel something crystalline slipping and catching beneath the cloth. After five years in my dining room, it smells of dusty fabric, like curtains that need a good washing.

My mother learned to make a *faccia malute* by watching her grandmother Elvira Bello. Elvira was a midwife; she delivered babies and had "the gift." According to my mother, Elvira said her "gift" caused her "too much grief in her life." The nature of this grief, though, is left mostly to my imagination. Her husband died young, leaving her with three children under the age of five and little money. Did she believe her powers were the cause? Did she, as a young girl, cast a love spell to change her fate? I'll never know. Tangibly, all we have left of my great-grandmother are two black and white photographs, a few faded recipe cards, and an old home movie that we can't play because we don't have an eight-millimeter projector anymore. The intangibles are harder to catalogue – the angle of a cheekbone, the familiar, unconscious motion of a hand stuffing ricotta into a pasta shell, and the ritual of the *faccia malute* …

Both photographs show Elvira as an older woman. In one, she is holding a chubby-faced toddler in a light dress. The toddler is my mother, Elvira's first grandchild. In the other photo, she is wearing a housedress and staring directly at the camera. Her face is much like mine. Her eyes are deeply set in the same way, and her forehead is wide and square. Though I can't tell from the picture, I suspect a prickly growth of hair on her chin; hairs like the ones my mother and I spend much time plucking. Her body is stout and her waist, like mine, nonexistent.

Some may think it odd that recipe cards survived almost a century, but it doesn't surprise me. Food is very important in my family; recipes are heirlooms. These recipes are for fancy cookies – scalili, an egg cookie; tordelli, a wine cookie; and pieneilli, a tart filled with raisins and walnuts then dipped in honey. Basic recipes for pasta, meatballs, and tomato sauce were never written down.

As a child, my mother remembers helping to prepare Sunday dinner. Everyone lived nearby then, just a few blocks away, and the women would gather in Elvira's kitchen on Saturdays to make pasta.

Elvira's kitchen was divided into two rooms. In the smaller room, the pantry, there was still a square door in the outer wall where the iceman used to slide blocks of ice directly into the icebox. In the larger room, the women and children worked the dough on a butcher block table so worn in the center that Elvira didn't even need to use a bowl. She would mound the flour in the slight depression, make a hole in the flour with her fist, and crack the eggs into it. Once the dough reached the right texture, she would pass it to the women at the table who rolled it into thin sheets. The children helped to cut it into small squares for ravioli or larger rectangles for manicotti. Then the women stuffed each piece with ricotta or sausage, and the process continued batch by batch until there was enough food to feed everyone. All the while, a cauldron of sauce simmered on the stove, scenting the air with garlic, basil, and oregano.

My mother's kitchen is much smaller, with a counter instead of a table, but it is where I learned to stuff manicotti. It has changed over the years, but in my youth the walls were papered white with pastel green frogs on deeper green lily pads. Mom mixed the ricotta, parmesan, parsley, and eggs in a large blue bowl, cracking the eggs on the edge of the counter. We didn't make our own dough, but she showed me how to spoon the mixture into the tube of pasta, first on one end and then on the other. It's trickier than it sounds and required a twist in the wrist and coordination between both hands. When I finished, my hands were sticky with ricotta and egg, but I was deeply satisfied by these motions that linked me back generations.

The last time I made manicotti with my mother, not too long ago, I noticed that her hands looked older. The skin seemed thinner, stretched tighter, and the veins seemed bluer, more pronounced. Her movements were as quick as ever, but I felt compelled to really look at her. It's easy to notice the changes in the house; the kitchen walls are now covered with blue and yellow posies, but not so easy to notice the first hints of gray in her brown hair.

My mother has not shown me how to make a *faccia malute*, but she has revealed the secret ingredient inside the pouch – rock salt. Part of me doesn't want to know; learning would mean admitting that she won't always be here. She has shown me the bottom drawer in her dresser where she keeps the fabric and yarn. Hidden there, nestled under the material, is a white crocheted purse, and within that, the *faccia malute* Elvira made for my mother.

Christy Diulus

SECTION SIX

Who am I? Who are you?

Clever men create themselves, but clever women, it seems to me, are created by their mothers. Women can never quite escape their mothers' cosmic pull, not their lip-biting expectations or their faulty love. We want to please our mothers, emulate them, disgrace them, oblige them, outrage them, and bury ourselves in the mysteries and consolations of their presence. When my mother and I are in the same room we work magic on each other: I grow impossibly cheerful and am guilty of reimagined naiveté and other indulgent stunts, and my mother's sad, helpless dithering becomes a song of succor. Within minutes, we're peddling away, the two of us, a genetic sewing machine that runs on limitless love. It's my belief that between mothers and daughters there is a kind of blood-hyphen that is, finally, indissoluble.

Carol Shields
Swann

Growing Up Half Jewish

I thought the whole world was Jewish. In the Bronx, where I spent a quarter of my life, nearly everyone was Jewish. My father was. One of my two grandmothers was. There was not one, but two "Koisher" butchers on the main block near my house. At PS 64 on Jewish holidays, there were only fifty kids in our school out of a usual attendance of 800.

I went to my Grandma Goldie's third-floor walk-up apartment every Friday to celebrate the Sabbath. My sister and I often accompanied her to the live Kosher chicken market where she picked out the unfortunate victim which was to become the centerpiece of the meal. Grandma Goldie also prepared gefilte fish and matzo ball soup from scratch and lit the Sabbath candles. I don't remember any of the words of blessing, but to this day, I use her recipe for garlic dill pickles.

In those days, people wanted to be "real Americans" and spoke little about the life left behind in the "old country". Grandma Goldie came over by boat through Ellis Island with two of her sons, one of whom was said to have been thirteen pounds at birth as compared to a sack of potatoes. Her other two sons, including my father, were born in the U.S. As unthinkable as it is to me now, she never saw her parents again after she left. My grandfather, Itzick, whose name is remembered in my middle name, Isabel, died falling off a ladder while painting houses. He left his wife with four small children to manage on her own.

My favorite part of the day as a child was walking around the corner to the stairs of the Jerome Avenue elevated train, to meet my father as he returned from work. I waited impatiently as each train roared over my head. I would have covered my ears but usually I had a sour pickle in each hand. The one with a small bite out of it was for me. The one for my father was still whole. Both were purchased for a nickel from the nearby pickle man whose smelly, waist-high barrels were filled with cucumbers in various states of decomposition.
Iris, Rebecca, Harriet, and Deborah were my friends. Not a Christian among them. I was the only shicksa at the bar mitzvah of my friend Steven Cohen. I was billed as his girlfriend much to the chagrin of his mother.

Sometimes, I rebelled against this atmosphere. At Christmas, my sister and I boldly set up a nativity set, lights and all, in the large, first-floor bedroom window of my apartment. On the High Holy Days when everyone paraded in the streets dressed in their finest, I incurred some disdainful looks when I dressed in dungarees.

I thought Grandma Goldie would always be there. Unfortunately, she moved to Florida when I was ten years old. I saw her rarely after that. She is standing in the front row of my wedding picture with her nylon stockings rolled up below the knees. Her last visit was soon after my first child was born. Grandma made her famous matzo ball soup which gave my Irish husband a heartburn that he will never forget. She also washed the floor in my kitchen and then put newspapers down immediately, leaving newsprint all over the beige tiles.

First communion, confirmation, and years of after-school religious instruction could not get the Jewish out of me. My close friend Linda tells me that I am the most Jewish Catholic person she has ever known. People routinely wish me *Shana Tova* (Happy New Year) in the fall on Rosh Hashanah. Ironically, or perhaps understandably, two of my three children converted to Judaism despite having been raised as practicing Catholics. Four of my six grandchildren are Jewish as well. The oldest is soon to be bat mitzvahed. My father and Grandma Goldie would be so proud.

Jane I. Cash

Good-Woman

When I think of a woman who has influenced my life, I think of *Good-Woman*. She is a composite of three women in my early life who have made me the person I am today.

My mother, the best homemaker I have ever known, is responsible for any housekeeping skills I may possess. She taught mainly by example as she didn't care for anyone "messing up" her kitchen. I was relegated to setting the table and stirring things on the stove. Her greatest gift was for hospitality. I had a couple of aunt and uncle combos (two brothers had married two sisters) who would drop by unannounced on a Sunday afternoon and were invariably invited to stay for dinner. My mother would send me to the cellar where there were canned fruits and vegetables. There was usually a roast in the oven on Sunday and with the addition of the jars from the cellar, a wonderful meal would appear.

Mother was a quiet lady who expressed love by "doing" for people. She worked as a practical nurse and I often ran into people who would praise her kindness and compassion even years after she cared for them. She had a no-nonsense side of her also. I remember whining, "I don't feel good." I was hoping she would say, "Oh, you need to stay home from school," but she never did. She would say, "Well, you know how you feel," handing the decision to me, but managing to imply that I was not sick enough to miss school. When my father had been drinking and coming and going, roaring the car engine and almost driving into the house, she would tell me to stay out of his way. Once he left again, she would make popcorn or dish up ice cream as a comfort measure. My sister Donna blamed her later problems with her weight on those occasions.

The next woman who is part of my ideal *Good-Woman* was a friend's mother who hauled me to Sunday school and later to play practices and other school activities. My mom did not drive and it wasn't until I had my own children that I appreciated this woman's kindness to me. I lived several miles out of her way, but if she heard I needed a ride, she would come. She was a Christian woman who knew of my alcoholic father and some of the problems in my family because of that situation.

My sister Donna represents the third aspect of *Good-Woman*. Eight years younger, I was often a thorn in her side. I would fall asleep in the car and lean against her. I can still hear her saying, "Get over; your feet are on me!" One night she called me to her room and invited me to sleep with her. I was touched and honored until I heard some "scratching" sounds in the wall behind her bed. Even a bratty little sister is welcome when one is scared.

At a time when I was very busy with my four children and their activities, she advised me to stay close to my husband. She said, "Very soon, it will be just the two of you again." It was good advice and I followed it. My husband and I were married forty-three years when he died.

I felt like I finally got to know my sister Donna after my children were grown because we both finally had time to visit for a few days in the summer. She and her husband lived in Indiana, but would come to Pennsylvania and camp for a couple weeks. In the last few years, we spent many evenings sitting by the fire with me as close as I could get to the flames and Donna admonishing, "Con, you are going to catch your shirt on fire." At those times she was just my big sister again.

Donna won a week at an Indiana resort in 2006 and asked my sister Ann and me to join her there. Ann was also a widow by this time, so it fell on Donna's husband Jim to graciously chauffer us around the countryside to antique shops and other local attractions. I learned things about my family that week that I had never heard – things that happened before I was born or when I was too young to remember. We celebrated Donna's birthday on that trip.

One morning Donna had an episode of nausea and vomiting. After a while, she insisted that she was up for whatever we had planned. Less than a month later she was diagnosed with pancreatic cancer and she showed the same courageous attitude through all the treatments that followed. I was able to go and help care for her a couple of times during her battle and I remember one of her daughters telling me, "I don't think Mom realizes what is happening, and I wish she would talk about it." When we were alone together, however, Donna looked at me with her clear bright blue eyes and said, "What do you think the end will be like?"

I miss her very much.

I think I have turned out pretty well, although there is plenty of room for improvement. I still hold up *Good-Woman* as a measure of my performance.

Connie Cousins

My Dear Little Girl

The following two items were discovered in my grandmother's (Laura Abadie Mulkey, 1887-1972) billfold after she died, along with her social security card. These notes are from her mother, Sallie Beall Abadie (1867-1949). The first is written in pencil on fragile paper circa 1900.

Miss Laura Abadie
At Home
My dear little Girl
I can write things so much better than I can say them, and I wanted you to know I appreciate your sweetness and thoughtfulness for me and your going with out things, when you really need them so take this money, its my milk money and get you a pretty pr[pair] of ties for Easter.
Mama

Abadie family photo circa 1894. L to R: William, Laura, William, Marie, Sallie. It was Sallie who wrote the notes to Laura, her daughter.

Evidently apologies (especially written ones) were rare things. This note was written in ink on heavy plain bond circa 1910.

Miss Laura Abadie
My Darling
The grieved look on your face as you left me this morning has been with me ever since.
Will your Mother ever learn to give her advice in a more tactful manner – I wonder?
What I wanted to say was, that I feared the style of dress was such that it would only be appropriate for very elaborate occasions. And you had better think it over more fully before putting $12. or $15. into it and feeling afterwards that you might have used it to better advantage.
I will phone Irma that you can't be there today – but for my sake,

please decide to do just what you yourself want to do – irrespective of any ones advice.
Mother

Thank you dear, for phoning its all right now

Dear Laura,

To quote my great grandmother Sallie, perhaps I, too, can write things better than I can say them.

You made me a mother – me, a somewhat lonely young woman 400 miles from home, with your father working very long hours. You were born simultaneously with his new "penny saver" newspaper. His workdays were very long with lots of financial pressures, which I did not appreciate at the time. So you and I lived in the drafty old house, for each other. When the marriage failed, our relationship intensified.

I worked part-time, taking you to the sitter in the morning and picking you up at noon. The rest of the day was ours. I sewed most of your clothes. We played with your toys and read your books. At night, you loved to hear *Winkin and Blinkin and Nod* or *The Gunnywolf*. You struggled to sleep through the night for quite a while. I would check to see if you were all right, then tell you to go back to sleep. I would lay awake listening for your pleas/cries to die down.

It's so hard to know what is right. I did the best I knew. When I first brought you home, I wondered what I was supposed to do with you until you were ready for kindergarten. Very soon, I couldn't imagine life "before Laura."

We traveled a lot in your first thirty months – flying to spend Thanksgiving of 1972 in Los Angeles with family. Grandma was there. On our return, we landed at Newark during a snowstorm, and I barely managed you and the large Samsonite suitcase loaded with Mexican tiles for the kitchen backsplash. Our housemate Kathy did manage to pick us up after ditching one of our cars at the bottom of Willow Tree Road, walking back uphill and trying again. I don't know HOW I would have managed without her picking us up, but I had never given it a thought!

Accepting another into our household was hard for you. You were two when we met Fritz. I had spoiled you, and as fathers are sometimes known as "reality figures," there were some rocky times.

Again, your world changed when you got your first two-wheeler at the end of first grade, as well as a baby sister. You were a big sister!! Now you had to share, and help, and clean up, and wash your lunch box, and get yourself dressed, waiting and shivering amid two-foot high snow banks for that school bus.

You grew independent of me and drove with your grandparents to their new house in Texas after vacationing in Ocracoke. You flew alone to attend the dedication of a Fort Worth orphanage with extended family.

You invited me to learn a new mother/daughter relationship in Elsinor and Copenhagen – the worldly teen/adult ushering her mother and aunt through Danish streets, shops, train routes, and host family meetings. For me, that was the most outstanding example of our role reversal, which has subtly increased over the years. In many little ways – your fashion tips ("Mom, after you tuck in your shirt, pull it up and blouse it a bit."); your gift of the "worry doll" from Myrtle Beach after Spring Break – you have eased my mind, soothed my soul, and boosted my ego. You listen with patience to my petty, daily annoyances at those I love, rarely burdening me with the stresses of your own challenging life.

I am blessed to have you.

Love,
Mom

P.S. – Wordsworth said "The child is father of the man." Thus, when you made me a mother, I began to know my mother and began to understand another aspect of life.

Sally Eckert

Pumpkin

Tonight, sound and light fracture into rain.
I carved my pumpkin too early for Halloween,
its concave face softens beside a row of rosemary.
I water the row, sometimes.
I have to relinquish the face to find flesh, bake the pumpkin.

Rosemary is a barky, needled shrub.
Mom says, "Use it for cooking sauces, roasts,
eggs; crush the leaves in your palm."
If I don't crush the needles they cook rigid, unappetizing.
The oven timer goes off, tells me the flesh is caramelized.

Grandmother Mary's box of recipes
is decorated with carved roses and grease fingerprints.
She no longer cooks complex meals;
candy wrappers claim her.
Mary stays indoors when it rains.

Mom isn't hers. It's obvious when you see them
in the same room. Mom's hair is pumpkin
spiced with nutmeg, paprika, cinnamon.
A tall glass of water is one of her constants.
She sips, says, "Bodies are so much water."

Her body is my absolute. The freckles, scraps of sun
or ocean salt. With her red hair, my father called her Pumpkin.
I know him by her stories, as if each one condenses
into an ingredient she measures without cup or spoon.
She knows. To see her smile, makes him real.

To hear he fell in love with her when she was Marion,
is hard to understand. I only know her as Mom, as Mavi.
She changed her name when she met her real, oyster-eating mother.
I braid her hair; my hands pick up pie crust scraps.
I miss those I can never meet.

Elizabeth Ashe

Recovery

It was an apocryphal tale, told to me during my growing-up years in Newark, New Jersey, that for the first five years of my life, an only child in a small railroad flat in Brooklyn with Grandma, Mother and three uncles, I had spoken Yiddish. This story was a mystery to me, and so was Grandma. A six-foot-tall photograph of my grandfather, heroic in his WWI uniform and taken before he brought his wife and children over from the old country, hung in our living room. But Grandma's story, when (if ever) represented to outsiders was a composite of unsubstantiated anecdotes from relatives for whom English was a second language. She herself refused to speak English.

When my father returned from the Navy, the three of us left Grandma and moved to Newark. I was told that Grandma didn't want to leave the old neighborhood. A short, stocky woman in handmade clothes and sensible shoes, she had long, dark hairs growing from her chin which she implored my mother to cut during our infrequent visits to the single room she had taken around the corner from her old flat. She would sit for long hours, silent, her hands folded in her lap, thumbs circling; and my mother would cry.

Some moments were reserved for me. As Grandma rocked, my mother would tell me stories of innocent villagers fleeing from bad people on horseback. To me, these were clearly fairy tales like those read to us at story time by our librarian in Newark. As an American child being groomed for college, I took my cues from my father who was born in the U.S. and a veteran of the Second World War. I learned to keep my distance from what he saw as Grandma's superstitions, unrealistic fears, and guilt-inducing silences. He confirmed for me what I had always seen as mysterious and questionable in Grandma's behavior: burying dinner utensils to make them clean? Refusing to leave a poor and unsafe neighborhood? Insisting that she came from a place called "Checkanovitz" when everyone I spoke to declared that there was no such place?

Years later, studying at New York University and celebrating my escape from Newark to a fashionable apartment in Brooklyn Heights, I took singing lessons for a brief time with a master of jazz improvisations. I found myself humming a Jewish melody I had been unable to retrieve for many years. I asked my teacher why he thought I hadn't been able to remember it. His dry, laconic reply: "Obviously, it wasn't very memorable." He was mistaken.

That year saw the onset of a profound emotional crisis in my life. After weeks of sleeplessness, in less than a moment, like a TV screen gone to snow, my visualizations of my past and all the people in it winked out ... pulled into a black hole and extinguished. In time, whenever the shutters clicked open again, my clearest, most poignant memories were those of my grandma: her soothing lullabies, her pretty face, her anxious rush to "close the lights" before the Sabbath.

And an uprising of fragments of Yiddish, recalled in lyrics, in dreams, in poems that seemed to write themselves, in melodies in minor key that restored my self and my history.

Over the course of the years during which my life was reconstructed and re-animated, fable became biography. I learned that the bad people on horseback were Cossacks and that Grandma had escaped from a pogrom in a village where people thought that long, dark chin hairs and Jewishness were signs of witchery. I learned that Grandma could have moved in with us, but that my father had objected and won out over my mother's protests. One day, decades later, shopping for my home in Connecticut, I asked the Polish salesman if he had ever heard of Checkonovitz. "Of course!" he replied and he directed me to a website which reads, "We Remember Jewish Ciechanowiec ... the Shtetl Which Once Graced this Earth and is No More."

Of the memories restored, the earliest were the most precious: I am four years old, standing with my grandmother in the old railroad flat. I am holding her hand and asking her what my mother and father are doing behind the curtain that separated the rooms. She is explaining to me that they love each other. Had I asked in Yiddish? Did she answer in Yiddish? I know now there must have been many other such moments.

For Anna Siegel

You called my name in a language I'd forgotten.
I thought it a reproach and left too soon
I thought that stubborn pride lit your candles, made you mute.
When I went dark on the Sabbath and lost my music
I knew then it had been fear.
Then I knew that when you were sad, you were grieving
And when you were alone you were frightened.
And left to die, you did as you were told.
Call my name now, Grandma,
    I have been good,
    I have been quiet,
    I have buried all my spoons.
Call my name ... we will sing together ... I will brush your hair.
    Zug mein numen Bubba
    Ich bin daw.

Marilyn Silverman

Sweet, Sturdy, Thrifty, and Original, Caroline

Caroline Galletly Glorie was a child of the Great Depression. She knew many ways to save money, including turning the thermostat down in winter, putting every empty can or bottle to some practical use, and creating gourmet options on the salary – and later, the pension – of a county worker.

After she retired, Caroline worked part time at a local antique shop, more for the fun of talking about her antiques than for the commission. Around this same time, she changed her name. She told us that she was always teased as a child with the harsh rhyme of "Caroline, Caroline! Soak your head in turpentine!" So, she changed her name to the softer sounding, "Carolyn." She made an exception when Neil Diamond's song "Sweet Caroline" was popular; then, she was Caroline again and loving the attention!

She may have had many thrifty habits to meet her needs, but she also got what she wanted. When we asked her where she got this antique or that quilting tool, she would proudly tell us about her self-proclaimed gift-of-the-month club and defiantly let us know that she deserved it. Sometimes she would follow up one of these explanations with a solid punch to my shoulder! She became a single mother and moved into a tiny house, inherited from her recently deceased, reclusive Uncle Freddy, when her husband's alcoholism turned violent. She created a charming home with little nooks decorated in colorful fabrics, weathered barn siding on the walls in the dining corner of the living room, and a non-operational, triple-seater outhouse in her back yard. She would have collected more of these bulky antiquities, but she could fit only one in her backyard. She collected other outhouses with her camera, and hung an outhouse calendar in the kitchen.

From her depression childhood and her sense of adventure, she transformed every challenge into some unique occasion for fun. This made her a very entertaining grandmother to my sister and me. When we visited our Grandma Glorie, she would motivate us to wash our hands before dinner by telling us to secretly choose a scented soap and she would then guess which soap we had used. There weren't many choices, and the only way to win was to use the unscented Ivory. There were few games to play at her house, but we enjoyed a barrel of monkeys and the ever time-consuming "match the buttons" game. Trying to find and organize similar buttons in Grandma's big button box could keep us occupied for at least an hour. A typical craft project would start with an empty soda bottle. We would cover it with masking tape and stain it with shoe polish to create a vase for Mom.

Second only to thrift was her attention to healthy eating. As a child she had recovered from tuberculosis with a damaged lung and she put a priority on simple, healthy foods. Her bread pudding with cinnamon and raisins was my favorite. She would often bring dried fruit including bananas and prunes for snacks on our adventure days. One of her questionable experiments was low fat, sugar-free chocolate chip cookies. We were sometimes the recipients of large blocks of government surplus American cheese that came in a plain package, but made very tasty grilled cheese sandwiches.

Caroline enjoyed life's simple pleasures: providing a home to a bird, feeling the sun's warmth, and watching clouds create patterns. She was fond of picking and photographing flowers along the side of the road; Queen Anne's lace and purple loosestrife were her favorites. She took us on many adventure day-trips exploring the Hudson Valley. She would pack a picnic lunch and off we would go on a Hudson River cruise or hiking around the mountain lakes: Minnewaska, Awosting, and Mohonk. When I was in high school, she took us on the sloop Clearwater, and, as a result, I later spent a week volunteering on the boat. I wish I had known that the popular guy who visited one day was Pete Seeger!

As a younger child in a large family, Caroline never really knew her older brother Arthur when she was growing up, but they bonded in their curious retirement activities. His free spirit helped her find her own independence on the open road. He took her on an annual pilgrimage to his recycled wood shack (including reused nails) on South Padre Island, Texas before it was a spring break haven for college kids. They traveled with his dog-pound sidekick, Texanne, who rode beside him in the truck or in a milk crate on the back of his motorcycle. Their lodging on the road was economy-class: pulling over on the side of a country road for the night.

As a teenager, I was very surprised to find out that Grandma had a boyfriend! George was a special companion who took her dining and dancing at their favorite social spot in Greenwood Lake. He made her very happy while they were together and she was devastated when he died.

The last quality time I spent with her was when we danced at my wedding while "Sweet Caroline" played in the background. She died soon after that, but her influence continues. The adventures we shared inspired my lifelong interest and career in environmental engineering. Her colorful quilts keep my two daughters warm and secure. My wife will testify that I've inherited Caroline's thrift as well her interest in the outhouse updated, of course, to an environmentally friendly, composting toilet in the backyard. Thanks to her, I try to instill the enjoyment of simple pleasures and outdoor expeditions in my children and they, too, seem to have her delight in looking for worms, getting muddy, and approaching all of life as an adventure.

Douglas James Glorie

Wealthy

My mom was only twenty-three when she had me. I don't think that I would have been able to handle being a mother at twenty-three, but, by that age, my mother was very well-prepared.

She grew up in a farming village in India. They had very few possessions and even less money. Every day when the children came home from school, they had to wash the one pair of school clothes they had so they could wear them again the next day. She was the eldest child of eight – three girls and five boys – and my grandmother's first and best helper, even starting school late because she was needed at home to help with her younger siblings.

As the oldest, she had a special place in their household. All of her siblings (to this day) look up to her. She was considered everyone's favorite, especially my grandfather's. When she finally did start school, she always earned top marks. Though they couldn't really afford it, her family decided to send her to college, going so far as to take out small loans to pay for her tuition. I find this just so amazing. It was very progressive to go through such pains to put a daughter through college (especially with so many other children at home, including boys). Most of her contemporaries were being married off. She was the only one in her family who did end up going to college, Gujarat University.

It was there that she met my father and married and soon after, they had me. My father had the opportunity to come to America to work for the Englehard Corporation, and he left his bride temporarily in India for this career advancement. My mother and I joined him in Jersey City, New Jersey when I was about a year old.

As I was growing up, I remember thinking my mother was the most beautiful woman in the world. She had big eyes, high cheekbones and a slender, elegant frame. I have always wished that I looked more like her, but everyone always said that I looked more like my dad (which I have to admit, is true).
She was a very hard worker, with a full-time job, even when my brother, two sisters, and I were little, and also ran most of the household. She was always a passionate person – a typical Aries – outspoken, fearless, and energetic. We often butted heads when I was a teenager and she once told me, "I hope you have a daughter one day who is just like you!" I find it ironic that we all share birthdays in April now: my mother, my daughter, and I are all fiery Arians. She got her wish, I guess.

She taught me so many things over the years; how to cook and put on a sari and speak in my native tongue. I've admired her for her beauty, her intelligence, her hard work and her ambition, but the feature I most admire is her generosity. She and her entire family are generous to a fault. Throughout my whole life I've watched her give

Mom, Dad, and baby Kirti.

things away. If someone admires something she's wearing, she will take it off and give it to them on the spot. She is constantly gifting people, sometimes people she barely knows.

All her brothers and sisters are exceptionally generous. Many times when I was a child, they pressed money into my palm for some reason or other, or for no reason at all. Even now, as an adult, they give me or my children money and gifts all the time. I often wonder what it is about them that sustains the family trait of generosity. It must have something to do with how poor they were as children. They don't look at money the way other people do. They don't live in fear of losing money because they didn't have much to begin with. They have survived, and even thrived, and know it wouldn't be the end of the world if they didn't have it anymore.

Just like everyone now, I worry about my job, my home, my savings. I wonder what the future holds. But then I think of my mother and her family who did so much with so little and I know that I, too, will survive no matter what. If I have my health, my mind, and my family – well, there is nothing I won't be able to do. Rich or poor, I will always be wealthy.

Thank you, Mom, for the wealth of spirit you've given me.

Kirti Patel

SPS

On occasion, my mother used to come out with the expression, *"SPS — Self praise stinks."* For my mom, even the word stinks was somewhat of a stretch beyond her comfort zone, so this harsh slogan would come out with great effort and much more disgust than any mere action of her oldest child (me) could have inspired.

This emotionally charged phrase made a deep impression on me in my childhood and adolescence, coming infrequently enough to catch my attention, and with such force as to convey a crisis of sorts. I'm not sure I even grasped exactly what self praise would sound like.

As I think about my mother spitting out these words, I now wonder in what context *she* heard and absorbed this message. Anna Vincenza Alessi was brought to the U.S. from Sicily as a three-year-old child when her father finally gained his U.S. citizenship. She grew up on the Lower East Side of Manhattan as a bilingual child whose parents worked in menial tasks. Grandpa Gabriel Alessi worked in the laundry at Belleview Hospital, and Grandma Nina washed the hallway floors in their building on the corner of Thirteenth Street and First Avenue. My mother's generation became upwardly mobile through the garment industry in New York City. When Anna quit high school at sixteen, it was to take a good factory job sewing women's clothing.

Perhaps she learned the phrase SPS from her own mother or father? Not likely. My grandparents spoke only minimal English their whole lives. Possibly from her older siblings? Hmm. I think Uncle Steve adored his youngest sister, but what about the middle child, my mother's older sister, Rose? An older sister might say such a thing to curb her younger sister's development as a rival. I can imagine that happening. What I can't remember at all is the situations around which my mother would use the phrase "SPS: Self Praise Stinks" with me.

I was the oldest child of five and feared my stern father's loud voice and the threatened removal of his belt to punish one of us. My parents mostly used threats with us: I don't recall ever being hit with my mother's wooden spoon or my father's belt. My brothers may have deserved any blows they received!

I always wondered if it was just the female children in our household who heard this message or was it a non-gendered piece of advice in a working class, immigrant Sicilian family. My sister, five year younger, has told me that she does not recall ever hearing SPS. The slogans she remembers are, "No News is Good News" and "If you can't say something nice, don't say anything at all." Come to think of it, these expressions encourage silence as well!

Although I don't recall the context for hearing and learning the message about self praise, it certainly sank in. That much I know for sure! Years and years later, I had the opportunity to be mentored by a highly accomplished CEO. In one of our conversations, he commented that "women believe that career advancement is built on solid achievement and credentials; men know that it is more about self promotion!" What a revelation to me to hear the flip side of the lesson I had learned from my mother!

Ever since that conversation with my mentor, I have worked hard to articulate confident statements of my skills, talents, and achievements, although I always hear a little echo of SPS in the background. I also wonder what might have been different in my mother's life if she had not been exposed to SPS even more thoroughly than I was.

Josephine Carubia

Grandmother's Balcony

I am a mixture of the influences of three generations of women: my mother, my grandmother, and my great grandmother. My great grandmother influenced my mother a lot. It seems to me that every girl child has a special relationship and special lessons to learn from her mother's mother. This story shows how a child absorbs the flavors of other generations.

I grew up in a small town on the Mediterranean Sea in the south of Turkey, called Iskenderun, little Alexandretta. My mom worked full time, so when there was no school, my sister and I would spend our days in my grandmother's home.

My grandmother, Leman, was a housewife who raised four children. My mother is the oldest child. Grandmother was not the breadwinner of the family, but she was the head of the house. My granddad would give her all the money and she would arrange everything.

Grandmother's apartment was on the third floor of a large building. It was always crowded with guests, relatives, and friends. My favorite place in this apartment was the balcony.

Our city was a hot and humid place and there was no air conditioning, so we would spend most of our time, especially in the afternoons, on that balcony. My grandmother would host tea parties almost every day for my aunts and their friends and other relatives who were visiting.

I loved spending all day long in summer on that balcony. I sat there watching people walk by, waving my hands and making small talk with people. Everybody knew everybody in that neighborhood. For example, I still remember talking to the owner of the local bakery who used to ask if my grandma needed any bread for lunch. I was the one who would hang down the straw basket and then pull it up full of hot bread. I had my first romantic crush on that balcony. He was the son of the pharmacist and I could watch him making deliveries to customers and sitting in front of the pharmacy chatting with his friends. At 5:30 p.m. every day, I would be there, sitting in the corner of the balcony, waiting to see my mother walking down the street to come and get us.

My grandmother is the reason I love to cook. She used to make her own tomato paste. In summer, my responsibility was to mix the tomato paste which was left to dry in the hot sunshine out on the balcony. Quite frequently, while I was doing this, I would dip my finger in and taste the fragrant and delicious (and forbidden) tomato paste. Then I would stir the big bowl with a wooden spoon to cover up the marks from my fingers so that my grandmother wouldn't know. I'm sure she knew anyway. I loved watching her cook for the guests coming because there were always guests in the house and they never left without sharing home-cooked, delicious dolmas (eggplants filled with rice and ground beef) and helva (a desert made with flour and sugar). I would watch my grandmother mixing the ingredients rich with tomato paste, looking at her eagerly, hoping she would let me try filling eggplants with rice.

Sinem Turgut (center) as a child with her grandparents and sister.

My grandmother died in 1999 and I was not there. I was far away and couldn't visit with her while she was dying. Not long after, my mother and my aunt decided to sell that apartment. When I visit my hometown and see that building, I feel a burning pain in my heart for the losses.

If I could have a memento to remember my grandmother, it would be that balcony and all those summer days I spent there looking inward to learn my role as a woman and outward to the enormous world of grown-ups. Grandmother's balcony was even better than school for learning about life!

Sinem Turgut

SECTION SEVEN

Lost and Found

Not until we are lost do we begin to understand ourselves.

Henry David Thoreau

Irish Whiskey, Neat

I might be in an airport in Chicago, a hotel room in Tucson, or a Basque bar in Bakersfield, California, but if it is Saint Patrick's Day, my mind is elsewhere. It is cold in the place that I remember. April is not the cruelest month in Minneapolis; March is. The crocuses are yet weeks off, and winter lingers unpleasantly. It snows more this month than any other. There are dirt streaks on the intersection windrows and white salt marks on fenders and doormats.

On the north side of the garage behind my grandmother's home there is a miniature gulley of ice, fed by periodic roof melts which prepare the sunless strip for the moss that will grow there in summer's heat. The only hint of spring is the moisture sag in the aging snowdrifts covering the petunia beds.

The house is a duplex. It has a screened porch, and in coming months people will sit there on wicker furniture and listen to the Minnesota Twins on small radios in the cricket-broken silence of summer nights. The wicker furniture is now in the basement, a dark cellar shielded by foot-thick, stone-like blocks. The house has other anachronisms: stained-glass windows, steam radiators, a vast, uninsulated, stand-up attic with huge trunks closed with metal clasps; a grandmother's attic of memory.

For a moment, thoughts go back to Christmas, when the family converged on the duplex, and its rooms were piled with gifts. The tree stood before the windows looking out on the porch, and there was a fake fireplace, brought down from the attic each December so that stockings could be hung. Grapefruit halves topped with sherry broiled in the kitchen, and in the upstairs duplex, where I would someday live, another tree – Aunt Jen's – attracted the children. Underneath it, in hummocked cotton, lay a village, perhaps a dozen A-framed structures: homes, stores, a church. Their fragile, cardboard facades had small windows of thin, colored plastic in which glowed the back-light of Christmas-tree bulbs. There was a sleigh, and carolers stood under street lamps, shadowed by lights from the village.

The smells of sherried grapefruit are gone from the kitchen as I enter it now. There is a table in the corner; a canary cage suspended over it. The placement of the table allows only two people to sit in comfort. This is so because the woman who eats here day after day has been alone for most of her life. One of seven sisters (all of whom stare, tightly corseted, from a faded sepia photograph in her bedroom), she was abandoned by her husband early in marriage and raised a family on her own resolve. Behind the refrigerator is a mouse hole. Its occupant is company, as familiar and as anonymous as the cleaning woman who came to the house every week for thirty years and whose last name no one ever knew.

On St. Patrick's Day, at about 2:00 p.m. if it falls on a weekend and 5:00 p.m. if it does not, Claire Keeler will sit down at her table with me and politely refuse an Irish whisky offered neat. I offer again and she accepts. This is our ritual. She drinks and we have the same conversation every year: How are things in the Register of Deeds office in City Hall where she works? Things are fine. And her son, Tom? He will visit from New York City in late summer but will not stay. The sisters? Sue has a broken hip and Hae, a gentleman friend, both unexpected. Silence. Then she will glance pensively out the window. Icicles have formed on the new flashing that cost her $1,000. The seldom-used concrete driveway continues to crumble.

Petunias come to her mind now. The Irish whisky brings them. And with their flowers will come the wicker furniture and the porch.

The six Ronner sisters. Claire Ronner Keeler is second from right in the bottom row.

Will the Twins' pitching be any good? She doesn't think so. Another Irish whisky? Yes. Just a half. It is poured full. What about her neighbor, the avowed Communist on whom the FBI once spied from her bedroom window? Well, he cuts his lawn, keeps up his property, and refuses to sell out to developers who are pockmarking the neighborhood with ugly sixteen-unit apartment buildings. The refrigerator mouse scurries across the floor. Only the canary reacts.

It is muted, this March afternoon we share. We have another Irish whisky, which is never Bushmill's because she will not drink anything distilled in Ulster. And she has been told that Jameson's is owned by Protestants. So it has to be Murphy's or Dunphy's or Powers. "Is there to be a party upstairs tonight?" she asks. "Yes," I say, "a few people are coming over to observe the day."

Actually, about sixty are expected. The afternoon newspaper people will come, and as they leave about 1:00 a.m., their counterparts from the morning daily will begin to drift in. We will go very late, and she knows that. And she will sleep through it all because she is hard-of-hearing, and I know that. "Shall we eat?" she asks. "Yes, let's." So, having settled important affairs for another year, we eat in the half-light and quiet of her kitchen on March 17, watched by the canary and, I presume, the mouse. When I leave, she will wash the dishes and turn to her crossword puzzle.

Claire Keeler has been in the ground thirty-four years this Holy Saturday. It still snows in March in Minneapolis. I no longer live above her in the old duplex, which has passed into careless hands. But each Saint Patrick's Day, I sit down at her table and we have an Irish whisky ... neat.

Richard W. Conklin

My Mother's Arms

I remember climbing into bed with my mother in the early mornings as a small child, and cuddling with my face on her arm. Her skin was warm, and olive brown, fragrant and sweet like almonds, and so soft.

There is a photo of her, taken in 1960 in the kitchen before we remodeled. Her arms are raised in surprise or in mock protest. There is a stack of paper cups on the table: company must be coming, company which was a constant delight. As the oldest child of six in her family, and the only daughter with five younger brothers who all lived nearby, our home was often filled with the wonderful sounds of their laughter and stories.

Now the house has been sold. So many and so much are gone.

But we can become those we love and lose: my grandfather feeding the birds in the park, sparrows on his hands; my grandmother growing orange trees from seeds on a Bronx windowsill; my father telling jokes and then laughing until tears ran down his cheeks; my mother's grace and her warm arms.

We are all of the people that we love and lose. In our arms we carry their gifts, our minds are filled with their jokes and stories, we have their good company always near us.

Lingering in bed one morning not long ago, resting my head on my arm, I was reminded of a warm and familiar scent. Here it was, like almonds, my own arms.

Ann Seltzer Pangborn

Sanctuary on the Sapelo

A huge white pelican was the first bird I saw as we inched and bumped along the sandy and grassy backwoods road toward a point of land on the Sapelo River in Eulonia, Georgia. The bird opened its beak and displayed the deep pouch below. "Oh, that's why we say that pelicans deliver babies!" came out of my mouth spontaneously. As we tip-toed from the car toward the huge enclosure, we spotted three more pelicans; all of them camouflaged brown and grey among the shadows of huge live oak trees shrouded in moss and amid the "furnishings" of their home: dock pilings, pond, roosts, and a few small tree trunks. The enclosure was about the size of a tennis court, surrounded in all dimensions with wire mesh. The mesh on top blended into the foliage canopy because the Spanish moss hung from it, too. The ground was covered with white sand. All in all, a large, comfortable, and natural-looking environment. Mary Ann and I whispered as we walked cautiously and slowly along the row of these huge habitats. We had heard about this bird sanctuary as a result of my questions about the roosting of so many birds on the trees at the point of land that we could see from her dock on the Sapelo River. "It's private property, but they don't mind if you visit the birds," we were told.

When we walked away from the pelicans, we saw two hawks sharing their territory with three owls, one of who-who-whom, swiveled its head to follow our movements as we approached, stopped, and walked by. Beyond the hawks and owls were two magnificent bald eagles in their own protected habitat complete with stick nests on high platforms. We encountered no other humans, in or out of wire mesh habitat.

I love the smooth, sweet texture of the words *Sapelo* and *Eulonia* on my tongue. Hearing or saying *Sapelo* brings to mind Van Morrison singing "Tupelo Honey." Both words are full of soft vowels. Just by saying *Sapelo* and *Eulonia* you have repeated most of the vowels, in slightly scrambled order, except for and *sometimes Y*. So the words sound and feel familiar from having recited *A, E, I, O, U, and sometimes Y* countless times as a language learner until those auditory shapes are a constant poem, a nursery rhyme, a warm, soothing, lulling, sing-songy surround-sound. And that's exactly what it feels like – in all experiential dimensions, including sound – to be with my cousin, Mary Ann.

Mary Ann and I are grown women with children and grandchildren. Not only do we live nearly 1,000 miles apart, we live in different cultures: I'm rooted in the Northeast and she lives in the South. This distance alone is a source of rich family history. Many years have gone by without a word exchanged between us, not out of estrangement or ill-will, but because of the fullness of experience within our families and careers. We are making an extra effort now to get together once a year for a long weekend. It is like sliding a secret drawer back into a notched tunnel to complete a carved figure. When the drawer clicks in, the figure is seamless and the separation is erased.

We connect at the level of extended family histories, nicknames, childhood antics, family vacations, mysterious grandparents, medical emergencies, and uncannily similar chronologies of growing up in the 1960s, marrying very young and having two children each, divorcing, and launching late careers that still stretch toward our full potential. And spreading across all this, like a flavorful arrabiata, is our family food. If "you are what you eat," then Mary Ann and I are flesh and blood, bone and cartilage *family* in the best sense of the word.

We started talking about food soon after I settled in Mary Ann's car heading north on Route 95 from Jacksonville International Airport to "the coast," shorthand for the house on the Sapelo River and vast low-country marshlands of coastal Georgia. We picked up the compelling topic of family foods with chicken bones and over the course of four days we moved along to lamb bones, pork chop bones, chuck steak bones, and bone marrow. For variety we touched on chicken skin, pan drippings, drinking blood, and eating roadside weeds. In terms of how we cook today, we are both known for our tomato sauce and meatballs and for tomato salad with lots of "juice" for dipping.

Mary Ann's mother, Rose, was my father's older sister by about eight years. She was also my own mother's godmother, making her much more than a sister-in-law. In fact, she was the matchmaker who brought her brother and goddaughter together. Their extended families had been close in the village of Cianciana, Provincia de Agrigento, Sicilia. They remained connected as *paisano* in New York City. My father tells the story of holding my infant mother at her baptism in Sicily and saying "What a beautiful baby!" (*Que bella ragaza!*). He told us he repeated this sentence when, at his sister's urging, he visited her soon after returning from Europe after WWII. Families with this much interconnection have a lot of food in common!

Once we got started there was no stopping us. I commented on how, in our families, the women and children self-selected the bony parts of the chicken as their favorites. Men ate the "white meat," boys were conditioned to "want" a leg, our mothers might have a thigh, and the girls fought over the "tasty bits," the wings and the "little bones" of the neck and ribcage. Both of our mothers made a flavorful basting sauce of butter, oregano, and lemon juice seasoned with garlic and salt and pepper. Roasting chicken with this sauce made it crispy-skinned and especially flavorful around the crunchy rib and wingtip bones which might even be a little blackened from the grill or oven. My mouth waters just thinking about it! Girl cousins would claim the "little bones" quickly and chew the ribs one by one, sucking out all the flavor. Then we would dip our bread in the mixed pan drippings and basting liquids. Mary Ann tells me that, even now, her own children automatically put all bones on her plate at family meals.

All of us cousins, boys and girls alike, loved the part of the chicken that "goes over the fence last." It was never called the tail, and we never thought about what it was exactly. It was "the part that goes over the fence last," and we truly did fight over this bit of fat and bone. Aunt Rose would save these parts in her freezer for months until we had a family gathering and then she would baste them and roast them to a tasty crunch and serve a big platter of this aromatic delicacy to all of the cousins. We would count them out carefully so that we each had four or five to savor. If we were served this dish at the family's table in Aunt Rose's restaurant, the patrons would notice the spicy aroma. "What is that dish you are serving to those children? Can we order the same dish?" She never revealed the secret.

Once we got started on bones and who ate what parts of the chicken, we began to expand this rich goldmine of remembrance. We both had sucked the marrow and clinging strings of meat from lamb bones cooked in sauce. Mary Ann remembered pork chop bones while my favorites were the bones of broiled lamb chops. We both savored the long blade from a good chuck steak whose meat was mostly removed for our fathers. The image of our mothers spooning red "juice" from the roast beef into our open mouths – like little birds lined up for worms – was buried deep down in my memory, but Mary Ann brought it up to vivid daylight. That warm, slightly cooked blood was a family sacrament shared spoonful by spoonful every Sunday.

The intimacy of shared foods from our childhoods was a foundation for talking comfortably about so many other things. Each touchstone of the past was linked with its own time capsule now open in the present. Because we could talk about the agonies of displacements and loss one or two generations in the past, the illnesses and deaths of parents, and our own treasured memories of each other's mothers, we could examine current family issues, too. We chewed those little bones together; we ate the bitter dandelion greens gathered by our fathers, to our great embarrassment, along the roadsides; and we learned to love bread soaked in the bloody juice at the bottom of the bowl.

Nothing in our lives today can possibly be outside the scope of our shared family history.

Our memories and family stories frame a safe place to reveal and understand our lives, and we laugh and cry inside this sanctuary. Our female cousin-ship feels like home, but like a good home where wounds are healed and where validation and confidence are forged, it is also a launching pad where we recharge batteries for our next adventure, a truly moving and moveable feast.

Josephine Carubia

Reconstructing the Tower of Babel
in memory of Judy Sortman

"We sometimes congratulate ourselves at the moment of waking from a troubled dream; it may be so the moment after death."
Nathaniel Hawthorne

Au revoir ma Cherie, my grandmother, who opened a pool she stopped swimming in after her esophageal veins exploded as diabetes crept through each cell of life for nine years and sickness overtook years of jaune cookie dough sprinkles, vert foncé macaroni, cheesed to scent, which seeped, steamy, through walls in your house full of beautiful dolls and bakery goods; we had the smell of flour in our hair and a faith I can recall.

Tu me manqueras, my grandma, mother of four, and many years grand for only two young girls; you were good at that job, taught us to bake or knit, impressionable minds that managed growth in summers spent swimming, endless days, picked up sent off with a kiss to play with handmade Barbie doll clothes crafted from lace bridesmaid dresses, la couleur de la pêch,e later mauve after the preparation for her youngest daughter's wedding.

Mes maux de coeur pour vous, my grams, who watched one movie at least one hundred times full length, to appease me and my sister, let us munch, spoil dinners with les sucreries rouges; we snuck to the basement, threw boxed food over the pool table, cold air alive with flushed excitement, bedrooms chock-full of peinture d'or the color of Jesus' hair and have you seen that glimmer or is it dark and Middle Eastern does it look the way you hoped?

Je ne devrais pas être triste, my guardian; you know the difference now, a passage from war, violence and pain, into anything better, perhaps a place where the bleu azur du ciel shines bright like vos yeux bleu-vert translucides; you know the freedom of no earthly ties, no possessions bind your hands with earth; you lie buried below it, but have risen above its decay; does it feel better, that comprehension?

Je devrais célébrer, my angel, because you have saved me many times in nine months; stopped my tripped foot, watched the blade tremble across my rough skin; les baisses de cramoisy dripped down, but you prevented the next cut, let me change something else about my body to distract my eyes, coated with a hint of your wisdom, from disgust; you understand now, what it means to have believed.

Je suis jaloux et plein de regrets, grandma, of whomever shares days with you now; I wanted you to help me remember how to crochet, teach me to decorate a wedding cake, cousez le bel habillement – doll-size up to mine – and I wish I knew more about your childhood, my history, and I wanted time that allowed me to show you my written words, or that last day back, a kiss goodbye, which I missed.

Je souhaite que vous ayez parlé français.

Rebecca Miller

Second Chance

My mother Hong Heung Soon was the youngest of three children. Her father died when she was about eleven years old. Her older brother took such good care of her and the family that she was able to go to the very best schools in Seoul, Korea. Because of her education, she grew up to become a very liberal woman for her time. Not many women went to college at that time in Korea. She studied art in Seoul and later studied art in Japan also. This rare opportunity to be so well educated was the most significant influence in her life.

She got a job at the post office and not long afterward she met my father who was the youngest of eight children in his family. Most marriages in Korea in the 1930s were still arranged by family representatives, but she and my father dated and their marriage was not an arranged marriage.

They stayed in Seoul for a short time after their marriage and then moved to the far north of Korea near the border with Manchuria. At this time, all of Korea was under forced occupation by Japan. My father was in business producing fish oil for export to Japan.

Their oldest child, my sister who is now seventy-one, was born in 1937. My brother and I were also born during the years they lived in the northern part of the country, what is today The Democratic People's Republic of Korea, or North Korea.

In 1946, they knew they had to escape the area and get back to the southern part of the country where most of the family lived. They had to give up their land and left most of their possessions behind. They were able to take some fish products with them that they could sell to begin a new life.

They returned to Seoul and my mother's older brother helped them get started again. My father managed the post office, and as a result, the family was able to live in the building.

My mother was always more than a homemaker. When I was in grammar school my mother was the leader of all the class mothers. She would come to the classroom and help the teacher. Everyone was very poor and she brought milk and bread for all the children.

In 1950, the Korean War started. My father had business connections and friends in the North and was therefore a suspect of South Korean authorities. He was also wanted by the North Koreans. I clearly remember the day war broke out, June 25, 1950. I was nine years old and we were very happy living in Seoul. I recall that it was a Sunday and the sun was shining. My memories of that day include beautiful flowers in our garden. My father was a devoted family man and he loved flowers. His flower gardens were so beautiful that people passing by would stop to take photographs. We were very happy.

After that day, my father had to hide. It seemed that the armies were always fighting in Seoul. I think the city changed hands from the North to the South several times. We didn't know exactly what was happening except for the terrible bombs and destruction we could see everywhere. Suddenly, my father was gone. Many years later, my father's second oldest brother told us that he witnessed his brother, my father, being captured by North Korean soldiers. He followed them. They were rushing to escape themselves and eventually they shot and buried all their captives. I don't know if my uncle ever told his own mother this story; she was waiting for her son to return for many, many years.

Of course we didn't know this at the time, and my mother would search for him everywhere. I remember one day when she and I and my brother went out to look for his dead body among all the people killed by bombings. I have vivid images in my brain of her turning bodies over in the street so we could see if one of them was our father and her husband. The city was flattened; nothing was left, just ashes.

After my father was captured, my mother was also in danger, so she changed her name to Tae Oak Youm and altered her birth date on official documents and left Seoul for about six months. We children lived with our mother's mother in her house. Our father was gone, and our mother was gone. We had almost nothing to eat. One day hungry North Korean soldiers came to our house looking for food. We begged them not to take our pet dog, but they took him anyway. As soon as they left the house, we heard a gunshot and we knew they had killed our dog for food.

After my mother came back to Seoul, in 1951 or 1952, we all moved to Tegu, the third-largest city in Korea. There she got a job with an American company. Eventually, we moved back to Seoul, and my mother continued to work for the American company and did well enough to send us to school. She always said to us, "If your father is alive, he will find us." That's how we knew he was dead, because he did not come back.

My mother always said she wanted to go to America to study art. She was very happy when I majored in art at Seoul National University. When I was in my third year at the University, she had a chance to go to America with her company. She moved to San Francisco when I was twenty-one, so it was about 1962. She began a program of art study in San Francisco and took a part-time job for an advertising agency. We were quite shocked that she was going back to school at her age.

After she graduated from art school, she worked as the creative director at an advertising agency. She had also become an excellent portrait painter and that's how she met her second husband, Tom. He was a very successful accountant who found it remarkable and lovable that on their first dinner date, my mother left nothing on her plate. They married in 1973 and lived on Baker Street in the Pacific Heights neighborhood of San Francisco.

My mother designed all the renovations for their home. The beautiful facade caught the eye of a film producer and both interior and exterior were filmed for the 1984 movie *Hard to Hold* starring Rick Springfield. Later they sold this house and bought a condo in the city and a sixty-acre vineyard in Napa Valley. It was an easy life of financial security, beautiful settings, comfort, and parties. Tom always said to us, "Since I met your Mom, my life has blossomed!" He treated her like a princess. This was my mother's second chance for a happy life. It was wonderful to see her doing design work, hosting parties, and enjoying her life far from the war zone and painful tragedies of her early adulthood.

Kyung Ryoon Kim

Hurricane Bob Salad, August 1991

If I knew you were safe,
there would be no need to pull the
vinegar, celery seeds, and honey
out of the cupboards.

How is it that this storm
provokes me to crush artichoke hearts;
to singe zucchini and shave carrots?

I can't even hear the wind from here,
and yet, I stab a plum tomato against a board
and dice the quarters into chunks.

You, of course, will know that this dressing
is made in a bowl full of vinegar,
which my mother said would eat my blood,
thus ensuring a lifelong courtship of
danger and piquance.
Is this the blend I hear in your voice, too?
"I'm so excited! It's my first hurricane!"

As I break the ribs of romaine lettuce,
and add oregano, just a pinch,
I picture you frightened, in the arms
of your lover and your friend.
I trust them to hold you now and rock you,
As mothers do,
And oceans would.

If God hears mothers' prayers
which take all forms we know,
this storm will seek its goddess
elsewhere,
and go.

Josephine Carubia

Une Grande Aventure

Living for eleven weeks in France (with my mother) was like being pregnant the first time: moments of feeling great punctuated by bursts of heartburn, frequent food cravings, astounding expansions of my waistline, and random mood shifts.

I broached the idea of living together in a foreign country to my mother when I began to consider what I wanted to do while my husband, Chris, a ceramic artist and a professor, took the last three months of his sabbatical living in the town of Den Bosch, Holland in the Spring of 2005. He had been accepted as a resident in a chi-chi ceramic artist residency program. The hitch? Families were not allowed to accompany the artist.

My daughters, Tori, age ten, and Rowan, age eight, and I wanted to be close enough to see him occasionally but also to have our own European adventure. France seemed a natural choice. I had a long-standing affinity for it, having visited twice during high school, and my mother has always loved all things French. So I invited my mother to join us. In semi-retirement, she was available and she could afford to split the expenses. The big bonus? As a long term Francophile, she was fluent in French.

On April 1, 2005, after a week visiting with Chris in Holland, and with huge bags in tow, the girls and I took the Thalys high-speed train from Amsterdam to Paris and met my mom at Charles De Gaulle airport.

"Ah, ma fille! Bonjour! Mes petites-filles, Tori et Rowan!" Are you ready? *Nous allons avoir une grande aventure!"* When my mom is happy her voice goes higher, in a kind of sing-song tone. Even when we visit her at her home in New York City, she often breaks into French; here it is a matter of course.

We kiss and hug hello. My arms reach easily around my mother. She's slim and has a petite build, unlike my more robust five-foot-eight frame, inherited from my father's side of the family. My mom has a kind of birdlike presence in some ways. She often cocks her head to the side as she considers something. And her movements are quick and bustling, though "efficiency in action" has never been her strong point.

She hates the wrinkles on her face, the thinning (she claims) of her hair, and as a consequence refuses to be photographed. But what I see when I look at her is a smallish-framed older woman with light blue eyes and graying light brown short hair. Her nose has a slight bend, but it's interesting, not unattractive, and with her high cheekbones, her face has a strong definition. When she smiles, it's a really wide, toothy, full-lipped grin and it's great! Her whole face lights up!

After our greetings and a quick café crème at one of the many small airport coffee stands, we make our way to the area where my pre-arranged leased car awaits.

"So, the car . . . it takes gas or diesel?" I ask the man behind the counter.

Not answering, he shoves the paperwork at me, pointing in some agitation to where I am supposed to sign.

"Uhh, *Monsieur, si'l vous plait, la voiture est* … " I stutter to a halt, having no idea how to continue, semi-amazed that I have stumbled out even these few words.

"C'est gazole! Gazole!" he says in a loud voice, as if that settles it.

"Oh. *Merci*." So which is it?

I sign the papers and call my mother in from where she is already instructing the girls on a few must-know French phrases. I need her to co-sign as the other legal driver.

I try a new line of inquiry.

"Monsieur. How do we get out of the airport and on the way south toward the Loire Valley? Do you have a map to show us the route?" I assume despite his single-minded use of French that he *must* be able to speak English. Who would put a non-English speaking person in charge of international leasing and rentals at Paris' primary international airport?

He responds in rapid French. *"C'est tres simple. Vous allez tout droite et puis, a droit, et puis, a gauche, et puis* … (blah, blah, blah …) *vous prenez la route A10! Ici!"* And he points to the map.

I tune out after the third *"droite"* (French for "right," as in right turn) assuming my mom is taking all this in. A few minutes later, climbing into our nifty Kangoo, I ask, "Mom, you got the directions, right? Other than a lot of rights and lefts, I haven't the faintest idea of where we need to go. And what did he say about *gazole*?"

"Well," says my mom, "I *think* I got the directions. But first he said we need to get gas."

"Why do we need gas?"

Mom turns to me. "The man said the car is on empty."

"What?" I say, flabbergasted. "The car is on empty? That doesn't make any sense. Can't they fill it here?"

As it turns out, no, they can't. Unlike the U.S., here you get your car on empty and then return it spitting fumes if possible.

The car, *la voiture*, is the cutest thing ever. The four of us instantly fall in love with it – small, compact on the outside, but remarkably spacious on the inside. It's a shiny blue-green. It's also a five-speed shift which

Tori and Rowan Staley with "la voiture."

my mom quickly informs me she hasn't driven in something like twenty years. It's clear that for today at least I'll be the driver and she'll be the navigator.

Thank god my mom and I both heard the man say *gazole* because, though it sounds like "gas" to me, it turns out *gazole* is French for diesel. Fumbling through a long sequence of figuring out how to open the little hatch on the gas tank and how to pay, we pull out for the open highway.

And immediately run headlong into chaos.

This occurs as a direct result of the man's pathetic directions and my mom's non-linear sense of navigation paired with transatlantic jet lag. She is seriously right-brained and since I already knew this, it's a complete wonder to me in retrospect that I let her loose with a map, expecting to get from A to B in a fairly straight line. It doesn't help that the rental agent said he didn't have a map of Paris. My mother took this news with remarkable equanimity, but I found it hard to believe for obvious reasons.

At this point, we are still on whatever highway the airport exit dumped us onto and we have gone past any number of exits. The exit signs fall into one of two types: 1) names of various towns across France, many of which seem bizarrely far away to merit mention in the Paris metro area; or 2) route numbers like A10 and N143, which change frequently without notice or simply end, and contain no helpful information on whether the exit will lead you East, West, South, or North on such-and-such route.

I am trying to hold onto a semblance of calm.

I am mumbling to myself now, "Remember, Kate, make this fun for the kids. It's just part of our great adventure, right?" I glance over to see my mother worriedly scanning the general map of France that we have, which is understandably useless in our present circumstances. Meanwhile, I am forced to go faster than I want to, like a guppy being carried along by a school of sharp-toothed barracuda; French drivers are just as insane as the stereotype about them claims.

We finally get off whatever highway we were on, and find a gas station with *une petite-marche*. Mom obligingly dashes in to ask for a Paris map and some directions.

We get lost before we can even find the highway again.

But this time, my mom saves the day and asks a driver sitting beside us at the next red light how to get back on the highway. He tells my mom – who translates for me – to follow him. We do, and miraculously, we soon find ourselves on the correct highway heading in what is clearly the right direction. Lacking any signs suggesting we are heading south, I am now cleverly using the sun's arc as a navigational aid, and we actually know what sign to look for next!

This whole little jaunt around Paris has taken us almost two hours, and we are no more than five miles from the airport.

Meanwhile, I am having that horrid, I've-got-a-gaping-pit-in-my-stomach feeling that if I can't understand my mom's somewhat slow-speaking request for directions or coffee or *gazole*, let alone personally ask for any of these, I am in ... (pardon my French) *profonde merde*. It is becoming clear that I have vastly overestimated the residue of French I learned from two trips during high school. In addition, figuring out in the of the next ten weeks of living together that at age forty, you are once again completely dependent on your mother for communicating with the outside world and navigating within it, is a very disquieting experience.

On the other hand, I know it's also true that if it weren't for my mother and her relative fluency, we might have circled Paris all night long.

Kate Staley

A Valentine Story

The year was 1904 when my parent's romance began. The handsome young man, Frank N. Gerhart, was a construction engineer with The Great Southern Railroad. He had signed a contract to lay the groundwork for a railroad between Danville and Harrodsburg, Kentucky. With one hundred men, one hundred mules, extensive equipment, and wagonloads of dynamite, I'm sure the encampment must have been quite impressive.

The entourage even had their own commissary. It was here that the romance began. My mother Mae Byrd Coleman, a lively beauty from Danville, was visiting a friend nearby. Mama and her friend accompanied the friend's mother to the commissary to purchase a roast for dinner. Daddy happened to be there.

There must have been an unbelievably magical connection between the two of them. Daddy immediately had a handwritten note delivered to Mama. Written on a brown paper sack, he asked permission to call on her the following Sunday afternoon. After consulting with her hostess, Mae Byrd answered, "Yes." So, of course, he followed through, presenting her with a large bag of beautiful fresh oranges.

May Byrd Coleman, age seventeen, in 1883.

Through that fall and winter, he spent Sunday afternoons with her at the family country home near Danville, always bringing a bag of oranges. Naturally, they became Mae's favorite fruit.

In the spring of 1905, Daddy's job was finished, and he was preparing to take a job in Greenville, Georgia. But what about Mae Byrd? Should he ride off into the Southern sunset without her? By now they had become very close. Both were avid readers and had an engaging sense of humor. They discussed their love of history, poetry, and horses, and shared a strong faith in God. How excited they must have been to share so many beliefs and traits!

138

As the time for Daddy to depart drew near, he decided he had better pop the question. I think, for one rare moment, Mama was at a loss for words. In her diary, she said she just looked at him tenderly and placed her hand on his. It makes me tear up just to think about it.

Their marriage took place in the family home, Coleman Heights, on June 27, 1905. In later years, I was able to visit this home, which was no longer in the family. Still beautiful, there were tall white columns out front, high ceilings, and many fireplaces. I can easily picture Mae Byrd regally descending the wide stairs, stepping carefully under the skirts of her white, dotted Swiss wedding dress. Daddy, entering from the back, was all dressed up, with the inevitable black bow-tie, his lifelong signature.

Theirs was a lifetime of ups and downs. Both were adventurous, but Daddy was a bit more likely to take a gamble. They never tired of talking to each other, and believe me, many of those discussions were pretty lively.

With the cotton and beef prices going up and down, some of his ventures didn't turn out too well. Although Mama grieved with him, she usually let him know when he blew it.

Let me tell you about the last time I saw them together. Daddy had been bedridden for several weeks. I was standing in the bedroom doorway when I saw them sitting on the side of the bed, arms around each other, saying The Lord's Prayer.

Within the hour he had gone to be with Jesus.
The date? February 14, 1949.

Hattie Mae Coleman Gerhart Johnson

Guardian Angel

Alzheimer's had taken away my aunt. All that was left of the woman who had once spoken two languages, had been the highest-ranking woman in a national company, a restaurateur, and world traveler was an empty shell.

It had been a while since I visited her in the nursing home. Walking down the hall I breathed through my mouth to avoid the smell of old people and urine. I spotted her sitting in a wheelchair in the hall with all of the other bodies.

I wondered if she still needed the glasses she wore? She couldn't read any longer and wouldn't recognize anything at a distance. Her face was still beautiful with only a few laugh lines around her eyes. Her once auburn hair was now pure white. She looked seventy, possibly, not eighty-six.

But the clothes were all wrong. This new version of Aunt Nina was dressed in a laundry-faded, cotton blouse paired with pull-on, polyester slacks large enough to go over the diapers that stuck out at her waist. Somehow the carefully selected outfits she arrived with had been lost in the home's crazy version of laundry bingo. Could this be the same elegant woman who once drove Cadillacs color-matched to her wardrobe?

When she first arrived at her new residence, a staff member had called to report that Aunt Nina had gotten into bed with a startled male patient. My cousin, her other niece, and I laughed because we knew she loved the attention of men. How could the memory of physical contact remain while she couldn't remember her own name?

I watched as she sat grinding her teeth. Gone was her wide smile and rich laughter along with her wonderful, sometimes bawdy, sense of humor. As I watched, I wondered if somewhere deep inside she knew she had Alzheimer's, and grinding her teeth was the only way she could release her rage. She had taken good care of herself, watched her weight, and kept her heart healthy so that, in the end, her heart beat strong in a mindless body, a placeholder waiting to die.

I recalled the fun times and laughter we shared on our trip to Italy, walking arm-in-arm not too steadily, through the streets of Florence after drinking at Harry's American Bar. Her words of wisdom and kookiness came back to me. She truly believed her long-deceased mother, father, and sister had returned to her as guardian angels and rode with her as she drove.

Three months later Aunt Nina's strong heart finally stopped and we gathered to say goodbye to the body that had become her prison. We dressed her in a beautiful, salmon colored, multi-pleated party dress she had saved for the occasion. There were many stories and lots of laughter – just the way it would have been if she were there. Finally, that gay, beautiful, laughing person had been set free. Free to be one of my guardian angels.

Darlene Throckmorton

Colored Circles

I was red, my eldest sister was yellow, my middle sister blue. Each chair, each bureau and table, each box was identified with a dime-sized sticker. Red, yellow, blue. Blue, yellow, red: rows of them on slips of waxy paper. Strange to think of my mother being reduced to a few sheaves of colored circles.

Although we had been back to Burkhardt Brothers only a few times over the last thirteen years since my mother died, the storage company had come to occupy intimate space in our emotional lives. It had become more than just the place we sent our monthly checks, attaching them with paper clips to the blue scripted letterhead of the family-owned company. It mattered, for instance, that a handful of the brothers had met my mother when we moved from our childhood house to a small apartment the summer before I left for college. And that, like most people who met her, they were charmed. With her halo of yellow curls, jeans, and sneakers, and this-is-me-take-it-or-leave-it attitude, she was hard to resist. Less than two years later, they returned to pack up all her belongings again but this time to store them in paper and darkness until we knew what to do with them. The fact that they had met her endeared them to us. We helped them pack, made them sandwiches and snacks, and one of them even crashed a year or so later on my sister's Manhattan couch. The stickers had been their idea; obviously they had done this kind of thing before.

It had taken my sisters and me almost a decade and a half but there we were, winding our way south from Boston in one rental car and one family minivan on our last trip to Burkhardt Brothers. We were finally ready to open our Pandora's box of grief and let it go. We had arranged to have a man meet us there with a truck and auction house expertise; there was too much for us to keep. None of us could remember exactly what was in the three fish-house-sized pallets and as the date drew closer we worried that the old Louis XVII English furniture and Dutch antiques, relics from when my mother's father was the ambassador to their native Holland, would be either worthless to Mr. Auction-House or worse, have turned to silt after years of neglect.

The original load to Burkhardt Brothers had actually been prepared by my mother and me. That summer I remember as especially long and hot. I'd ride my bike home from my busboy duties at a local restaurant, one that was patronized by rich ladies with too much time and red nail polish on their hands and managed by a corpulent Greek who daily beat his personal best in the drinking and shouting departments. Peeling off my wrinkled uniform each afternoon, I'd find my mother in some new corner of the house see-sawing between joyful nostalgia and the black sludge of a failed marriage, unknown future, and an imminently empty house. Although she was as ready for me to go to college as I was to go, we tread those months on fragile ground.

There seemed like an acre of boxes and furniture laid out for us when we arrived. The three cups of coffee I'd had at our father's and stepmother's house sank cold and acidic in the holes left empty by each positive peppy promising word I'd spoken to my sisters. "Sure, it'll be hard, really hard," I'd said. "But it's time. Mum wouldn't want us to spend any more money or worry-time on this. She'd want us to take a couple of things to remember and let the rest go." Rallying around them I felt like a hypocrite as I struggled to split the waves of depression – part of our mother's jumbled legacy to us, it sometimes seems.

Mr. Auction-House-on-a-Schedule helped us begin. We started dividing into groups armoires, coiffeurs, bureaus, bontierres, tables, chairs, and other pieces of furniture for which I don't know the proper names: Keep, Sell, Toss, Maybe. Some of the Burkhardts commented: "Oh, it must be like Christmas opening all this stuff up after so many years." I tried to smile and stay light. The cartons were strangely difficult to open even with the aid of a pocket knife and I couldn't help but wonder who I would be now if those boxes had never been sealed.

My mother's handwriting was on many of the boxes. She identified each with our initials and contents therein: "VLT BOOKS," "RST PHOTOS," "LST SCHOOL," "ENGLAND 1968-1973." The soft curves of her vowels and the ebullient slants of her consonants were spirited and strong like her best self. Seeing the faded ink reminded me of that summer before college. I touched the letters on the soft worn cardboard and wished I could ask her why she hadn't believed in herself.

Thirteen years is a long time to prepare for anything. My sisters and I had rarely been together, just the three of us, since she died. It was almost as if all that time in the hospital with her those last months had done us in. Her death had brought us closer, but in some ways, it also distanced us. We see her in each other and sometimes still it is easier to simply turn away.

Soon after she died, the three of us spent a few days together dividing up her belongings. Her apartment was suddenly enormous and we didn't quite know how to fit into this new role of adult to which we'd been instantaneously assigned. Our grandmother, our uncle and his wife were around briefly, and our father, stepmother, and tiny half-sister were one town away, but they were as separate a family as they had been since my parents had divorced some ten years prior. The flip-sides of those busy packing days were spent drinking too much wine and, for me, running too many miles and reading my college Chaucer and George Eliot in a blind frenzy.

"What's so funny?" I called to my sisters from my mother's closet on the second or third of those afternoons. I was sitting Indian-style amidst piles of silks and satins, wools and tweeds, shoes, bags, stockings. I had put on one of her favorite sweaters and pulled the turtleneck over my face. It smelled warm and lovely, a familiar smell which would soon fade like color in sun.

"Listen to this," Becca said.

"It's your kindergarten report card," Weez prompted. "Mum kept all of them."

"When asked what her favorite subjects were, Victoria enthusiastically responded: reading, writing, lunch, and sports," Becca read.

I shouted from the closet: "Let me hear one of yours."

Becca pulled from the pile. " 'Louise likes to socialize,' Miss Dowd wrote, 'and should try to apply herself better.' "

"Miss Dowd? I don't remember her," I said.

"Fourth grade. Greycotes," Weez piped up. "Those English teachers didn't care if you had friends or not."

Then Becca whooped: "Here's my French prize from Winsor."

"Oh, no … Madam Zombeck!" Weez and I said in unison.

We all bust out laughing. Rebecca had been very talented in French but part of her victory – and she was the first to admit it – was due to the fact that the chalk-throwing, B.O.-smelling French teacher had adored her best for her impeccable handwriting.

I looked beyond the heaps of lifeless clothes and remembered how comforting my mother had been when I returned in tears from school after my second day with Madam Zombeck.

"I see you are nothing like your sister," the teacher had said. My mother hugged me close and we both laughed. Like our approaches to life, she and I had similar handwriting: loose, free, and at times downright sloppy.

In one of the yellow-stickered boxes, Becca had come across that French prize tucked neatly under copies of *Candide*, *L'Etranger*, and *Les Adventures du Petit Nicolas*. She forced a jaunty squeal, but Weez and I were lost in the world of our own blue- and red-marked cartons. Despite the fact that we were surrounded by big pieces of furniture that had stood as long as we could remember in our house – inanimate members of the family – it was the sight of the small items which tethered me back to past landscapes.

One treasure I found was my little tin camping cup. We had lived in England and Scotland for four years when we were children, and in my mind, those years, in the first decade of life, equaled childhood. They were years of magic adventure and discovery complete with a cohesive and, I thought, happy family of five, dogs, a house-trained rabbit, and camping on holidays throughout Europe. That one tin cup picturing a dancing aardvark, fly, pig, and long-tailed grinning rat brought those happy times back. For me, childhood became something of a different beast altogether a year later back in America when my parents divorced, remarriages followed, step- and half-sisters entered the picture, another divorce was filed, then finally a death by deadly cells. I lifted the cup from the box and smiled at the two-stepping animals. Their tiny faces reflected the self I sometimes felt I'd lost somewhere in those messy years.

Where there is treasure, there is invariably trash. We found an old oak lap desk filled with matchbooks my mother had collected over the years. A treasure to her perhaps, but had we been spending thousands of dollars all these years to store enough matches to burn all of Burkhardt down? We also found a tarnished muffin tin in the top drawer of a bureau, an object that caused great amusement for the three of us since the minute the oldest of us could reach the knob to the stove, I don't think my mother ever again baked another cookie or muffin. We unveiled portraits: among many of nameless ancestors, we found one of my mother at about age thirty-five and one of the three of us, painted, if I recall, by an amateur-artist friend of my parents, a fact which upon first glance was none too obvious. Now, however, with time and loss the two dilettantish portraits had bumped up at least a few notches from trash to treasure.

With each box I continued to gravitate to books, Rebecca to furniture and objects of elegant beauty, and Louise – being the Earth Mother that she is – to the antique doll furniture. miniature cradles and bureaus my mother had refinished and given to us as presents over the years. We also discovered the whale mobile a fisherman friend of my mother's had carved for her, a complete set of Dutch-English dictionaries, and countless folders of loose photographs. In one box we found all of my mother's diaries written as a young girl in her native language, and then a few, in English, from our travels abroad. Unfortunately, as a young wife and mother she had kept her heart closed even from her own personal journal pages. The entries told of what we did, where we visited, and with whom we spent time. My sisters and I flipped through them for nuggets, hoping for an illuminating passage which would explain in one simple string of words the woman who was as strong as she was weak, spirited as she was defeated, infallible as fragile but invariably lovely and loving. In a smooth manila envelope we discovered two love letters from my father to her, and one letter upon their separation telling her he would always love her. The latter was clipped to a watercolor he had made of a landscape seen through a window. The colors were loose and ephemeral. Underneath in his small surgeon hand was written: "Another time, another place." I wrapped all the diaries together and placed them in a red-circled box marked *Keep*.

Our hours at Burkhardt were winding down. We stopped to exchange papers and estimates from Mr. Auction-House. It was all so business-like; there was no time, not even a moment, to let my eyes stare off and fall out of focus. However, seeing our furniture puzzle-pieced into the back of his truck, I knew then that for a long while to come each time I would pass an antique furniture shop I would hold my breath hoping I wouldn't gaze in and see something across which my mother's hands had often swept.

I can't speak for my sisters, but as Mr. Auction-House drove off, I realized for the first time how ready I had been to open up those pallets, go through our mother's life, our parent's marriage, our childhood. The day was more about release than loss.

"Look who I found!" Weez chirped.

Amidst some old toys my sister pulled out a lumpy rag doll. A lifetime ago the doll's face had been caught under the metal seat lever of our father's old Kharmann-Ghia and due to that famous accident had aptly been named Bashy. The three of us had to stop what we were doing to admire her. She seemed thinner and perhaps lumpier, but her face still had the sweetest expression. I had to take a deep breath; if I cried over Bashy, I knew that would be it.

We finished up the day dirty and drained. We each took a few pieces of furniture and several boxes of books, photos, and miscellany. Each of us already had some of our mother's things; and after all, things are just things.

We hugged the Burkhardt Brothers good-bye, baffled by a new sense of loss where we hadn't expected one, and drove off, Louise in her family minivan to upstate New York, Rebecca and I in our rented sedan to Manhattan.

It didn't come for me until a week later, and surprisingly, *it* didn't come for any of us on the Burkhardt day. Two weeks after our trip, finally getting around to unpacking the red-stickered cartons I had stacked beside my desk, the emotions came. Each book and object I pulled out smelled of England, of family dinners, of jokes and laughs and rituals, of our mother's yellow hair and long comforting fingers, of our father's read-aloud voice, of childhood glee, of future. I wondered what my sisters were doing and how their unpacking had gone. Had Louise cried over an antique doll cradle? Rebecca over Bashy's crooked little face? Thinking of them, I realized how unprepared we had all been for her death.

Inside the last carton, I discovered my mother's babyhood music box. A stout little metal cylinder with a painting on top, it sat dented and loved, the paint faded and chipped. I don't remember the circumstances under which she gave me that music box, but as a kid I knew to treat it like the treasure it was. I had always loved boxes and tiny found items for inside. Somehow there was a magic to boxes, possibility or potential, something forgotten to be found upon re-opening. The music box, although it didn't open, was full of that kind of magic. As a kid, I would turn the bent arm, gripping the bone bead at the top, only when I really needed to. When I was sad or lonely or when I'd read a story with characters so real they felt more alive to me than flesh-and-blood people, I'd let the music twirl out of the box and fill me back up.

I slowly turned the bent arm and as soon as the music started I knew once and for all, thirteen years after the fact, that my mother was gone. Caught between the little metal arm and the bone bead was a tangle of white blond hair, my mother's baby curls. Even as a child, I knew that turning the arm and setting that music free was as close as I could get to the essence of my mother's best, most pure, most complete self. As the music coiled out into the hinting warmth of spring, I realized that we had all overestimated the effects of time. As it turns out, it is that very passage that is the most precious gift.

Victoria Tilney McDonough

Christmas Socks

When we think of Christmas stockings we usually think of Santa Claus, Christmas decorations, and lots and lots of presents. We don't think of disappointment, anger, a sense of unfairness, or even a lesson in giving; at least I didn't think of such things until the Christmas of my ninth year.

The year was 1945, the year of our father's death in August. As a tribute to his loss, our mother, Mary, decided that there would be no Christmas that year in the Bellanti home in Wilson Borough, Pennsylvania. The mourning period was one whole year, a time to affirm a ritual of personal sacrifice, honoring the dead, letting go that goes back centuries among the Abruzzi people of Italy. The prospect of a year without celebrations felt like an eternity and I felt angry with the parent who chose this ritual over the immediate needs of the rest of the family. To my mother there was wisdom in this ritual. To us children, the funeral with all its incomprehensible traditions was more than enough time for grieving. Why should Mother require that Christmas be without joy?

Grandma Gilda also held this ritual sacred, but she understood that grandchildren had other wants and needs. The hospital and doctor bills plus funeral expenses had taken a toll on the family's finances, but Grandma bought us presents that year. She gave me three pairs of wonderful warm wool socks that came almost to my knees. They were replacements for my two pairs of socks with potato-sized holes in the heels. Since my shoes also had holes in the soles, the socks were a treasured gift.

When Grandma left to return to her farm in Raubsville, Pennsylvania my mother had other plans. She asked me to choose the pair of socks I liked the most. I chose the green pair. Then she said, "Okay, now wrap the other two pairs of socks in the same wrapping paper; we are going to your Aunt's home to give your cousins, Ernie and Tony, a Christmas present."

"Now wait a minute," I shouted angrily. "Grammy gave those socks to me. They are my socks, not theirs!"

"I'm sorry," Mom said, "You have more socks than they do. You don't need three pairs while they have less." The argument that followed was useless. Our mom was a forceful woman. The Baronesse had spoken and wasn't about to change her mind.

The months passed and I quickly forgot about the socks. However, the seed she planted that Christmas sprouted in a different form.

It was Thanksgiving 1951; I had been inducted into the Hi-Y Club, a service club for high school boys, stressing clean speech, clean sportsmanship, clean scholarship, and clean living. Part of my service responsibility was to be in charge of organizing a Thanksgiving basket for a needy family.

Four of us took the basket to a family of seven – an injured father, a pregnant wife, and five children. They lived in a concrete bunker ten feet wide and twenty feet long. A drab curtain separated the cluttered living room from the bedroom where all seven slept. A pot-bellied stove was in the middle of the living room where they cooked and created heat for the winter. There was no running water, no indoor bathroom. The family was so grateful for the food we brought, including their first home-cooked turkey.

As we left I regretted that we hadn't purchased more. As we drove home, I found myself thinking of Christmas 1945, and my Mother's actions.

I told my mother what we had done and the effect this service project had had on me. In those moments as we embraced there was a deeper connection between us. Mother had strong intuitive skills. As we looked at each other in silence I didn't need to mention what I was thinking; I knew that she had done her best to teach me the meaning of love in action – a gift even more precious than socks.

John Bellanti

SECTION EIGHT

Universal Singularities

*Today you are You, that is truer than true.
There is no one alive who is Youer than You.*

Dr. Seuss

We Don't Eat Shrimp

In my family, we don't eat shrimp. We eat other seafood, just not shrimp. We eat mackerel every Wednesday. Dad throws it on the grill. Mom makes French fries, and my sister and I cut thin slices of lemon to squirt on the fish. We eat sprat, too. It's a tiny little fish that hardly has any meat on its prickly bones. But we love it breaded and fried until it's crunchy like potato chips. We usually eat it during family vacations to the Black Sea or whenever we're near any big body of water, like an artificial lake or a reservoir, but really wishing we were at the beach. On December 6, we eat carp. All Bulgarians do. That's just what you eat on St. Nicholas day. If your name is Nikolai, or Nikoleta, or Nikolina – or anything else that sounds even vaguely like Nicholas – you stuff a carp with rice and vegetables, maybe some raisins if you are feeling adventurous, and you have all your friends and family over to celebrate. Carp is a bottom-dweller. It has big, thick bones and very little meat. You have to stuff it. If you don't stuff it, there's not much to eat. Shrimp, we just don't eat.

Mom lost her job in 1992. She had been working at the same electronics plant for upwards of ten years, so it came as a big surprise to her. She had really liked it there. It was a state-of-the-art facility producing knock-offs of Western micro-electronic components that would then be exported to other countries within the Soviet bloc. It was a good use of her degree (she had studied chemical engineering in the university) and she got to wear what looked like a white ninja suit. She liked her job because all her co-workers were engineers like her, and they got their monthly salary direct-deposited into their bank accounts. Most other Bulgarians had to stand in long lines to get their salary in cash and, after they had waited for an hour, the cashier would tell everyone, "That's it for today; come back tomorrow." Mom also liked her job because she made a lot of money doing it. She made more than Dad who was also an engineer but worked in a different plant. When she lost her job, she cried for weeks.

The Unemployment Bureau sent her to a continuing education course to learn about Microsoft Word. There were no computers in the classroom at the learning center, and the instructor drew command buttons on a blackboard with chalk. Then he would dictate orders of operation. "You make a selection and then you click on the 'cut' button, that's right, the one with the scissors that I just drew. That will remove the selected text from your document and make a copy of it on the clipboard. What is a clipboard? Well, that's a little hard to draw now, isn't it?" And so he would continue. When the computer course was over, she had no job, a husband with an average salary, two daughters, and no knowledge of Microsoft Word.

She took the first position the Unemployment Bureau offered her. It was a job at a nearby factory de-veining shrimp. The black vein of a shrimp is actually its digestive tract, and it is not necessary to remove it. It's perfectly edible, though some people swear it tastes gritty and dirty. It's a question of taste, really. At her new job Mom would sit at a long rectangular table with thirty or forty other women – engineers, physicists, researchers from her old job. She would have a big bucket of shrimp next to her and a small de-veining knife in her hand. She would pick up a shrimp, run the de-veiner down its back, and remove the black vein. One of her supervisors would yell if the women left the shells on the shrimp. The other would yell if they didn't. Removing the shells, Mom thought, was also a matter of taste, so sometimes she would remove them and sometimes she wouldn't. She did it with her bare hands since she wasn't allowed to wear rubber gloves. Both supervisors were convinced that one could not properly de-vein shrimp with rubber gloves on. When she would come home – quiet, stinking of dead shrimp – Mom would kiss my sister on her forehead, kiss me on both cheeks and then get into the shower. She would spend a lot of time in the shower. She never told us, and we never heard her, but we knew she had been crying.

Mom's fiftieth birthday was a couple of years ago. She had a lot to celebrate. My sister and I had both graduated from good universities. She not only had learned Microsoft Word but had gotten so comfortable using her computer that she no longer even bothered mentioning it in her resume. The sad years of early democracy were over and there was a big menu to be planned.

My sister emailed her suggestions from Bremen. I dictated my ideas from Pennsylvania over Skype. Dad polled both sets of grandparents and Mom wrote list after list of party ideas. It was such a special occasion, the consensus was that it required a special meal. Not simply pork, or chicken or vegetables. It had to be something more involved than that. Seafood, we all agreed, would make most sense for the occasion.

We bounced ideas back and forth for weeks but at no point did anyone suggest that we serve shrimp.

Petya Kirilova-Grady

One of a Kind

Being a child of the depression, my mother was very frugal. Really frugal. Ok, cheap. This used to embarrass me immensely. For example, my mother made all of my clothes when I was growing up. She sewed all of my dresses and knitted all of my sweaters. She was an excellent seamstress and knitter, but all of my clothes were made out of really inexpensive cloth. Once she made me a dress with flowers all over it, and the first time it was washed everything in the pattern that was pink literally disappeared. She would also occasionally take one of her own dresses that she didn't want any more, completely deconstruct it, and then use that material to make me a dress.

She did the same thing for knitted items. If my older brother outgrew a sweater, my mother would unravel the end and take it apart. She would then wash the yarn and reuse it to make me a sweater. Every year, I would get at least one "original" sweater that used all of the leftover yarn. I still have most of them and they are really works of art, although at the time – horrible! If she was knitting something that took two-ply yarn, she would buy four-ply yarn because it was cheaper and slowly separate it into two balls of two-ply yarn. This took hours and required team work, but she ended up getting about four skeins of yarn for the price of one skein.

My mother could also reupholster furniture in a really professional way – if someone wanted to get rid of a chair, my mother took it and reupholstered it to look like new. If flat sheets were on sale she would buy two and make one into a fitted sheet. She would make pillow cases out of old sheets, using the part of the sheet that wasn't worn.

She reused everything. After the last facial tissue in the box was used, she would carefully cut off the top and then use the box to store small items like curlers, bobby pins, and lipstick. My mother also bought the cheapest generic brand of anything. Tissues would practically rip your skin off when you blew your nose; shampoo would barely make a bubble. When I was instructed to bring a bar of soap in a plastic soap dish to gym class in junior high, my mother wouldn't consider buying a plastic soap dish when we had one that the dog soap came in. The plastic case actually said "Dog Soap" on it in raised letters and the soap that I used had to be cut down a half inch to fit into the box because a bar of dog soap was a little smaller than a bar of people soap. I still remember my gym teacher pausing outside of my shower stall laughing. She asked, "Who is in this stall?" I replied, "It's Alyce," and I heard her chuckling all the way down the row of stalls.

When I got older, I looked back and admired what my mother did – all of my clothes and sweaters were "originals" and now it's fashionable to "go green" by reusing and recycling and creating as little waste as possible. My mother was one of a kind and far ahead of her time!

The other day I took the cotton out of new bottle of aspirin and was about to toss it when I suddenly thought of my mother – I looked at it for a second and then decided that it would work perfectly fine to take nail polish off. I tossed it in the re-purposed facial tissue box that I now use to store my manicure supplies. She would have been proud.

Alyce Paquette Moore

I Married a Mother, 1991

Who would have guessed?
I married a mother,
Someone's mother!
I thought it was a woman
(which it was)
but a mother to boot.
I should have known,
the signs were there:
the station wagon
and her eyes escaping mine
to check the wristwatch.
I should have guessed,
the copy of Spock;
the curious items in her handbag:
bright plastic keys
and a pacifier –
those distant looks
that swept past me
to questions beyond my asking.
A mother,
someone's mother
fell in love with me!
I knew, when I knew,
that it was an honor
to have married a mother.

Fritz Eckert

The Bold One

My mother came from a large, loving family of French-speaking Acadians in New Brunswick, Canada. Her parents owned a beautiful farm. When my grandfather (Pépère) could not provide for the family by farming, he would come to the U.S. and work as a teamster. He would drive a team of horses hauling materials and products for factories throughout Massachusetts. His children – my mother and uncles and aunts – were born in all the places in Massachusetts where he found work. Several were born in Fitchburg, at least one in North Attleboro, and my mother was born in Somerville.

My mother Eva was the bold one in the family. In French, they would call her *effronte* or "fresh." She delighted in telling us this story over and over again in her native language. It took place when they were on the farm in New Brunswick.

Mother was about fourteen years old and she was walking home from somewhere with her best friend. She saw her father on the roof of the barn with another person. He was up there with his best friend, Monsieur Bourgeois, but my mother never had twenty-twenty vision, so she couldn't really see all that clearly *who* was up there. She made the assumption that it was the son of her father's friend, not the older gentleman.

She shouted up to them, "Hey! Monkeys really like being up there on high, don't they?" *Les singes aime don etre en haut, n'est-ce pas?*

Eva in 1929 at age eighteen.

Of course, when she got home that night, her father was not too pleased with her. My pépère was somewhat stern and this time she wasn't able to get around him.

He told her, "Tonight when Monsieur Bourgeois comes over, you are going to apologize for what you said to him this afternoon!"

A short time after dinner while they were clearing the table Mr. Bourgeois arrived. Pépère said, "Eva, isn't there something you want to say to Monsieur Bourgeois?"

155

My mother stood in the doorway with her hands on her hips, and in a clear loud voice, she announced, "Monsieur Bourgeois, I'm very sorry I mistook you for a monkey this afternoon!" Then she turned on her heel, and out she went.

Calling Monsieur Bourgeois a monkey for the second time wasn't really the apology that my grandfather expected, but Mother never told us what he said after she issued her cheeky remark.

I loved visiting my grandparents on that farm when I was a child. It was a ten-minute walk to the ocean. We'd cross the field of the neighbor's farm, climb over a little fence and there was the ocean. We would make the trip for just one or two weeks every two years. My mémère would be sitting there in her rocking chair by the stove. We all knew that she just couldn't let a child walk by without grabbing her for a big hug. She would call us these little names in French, "*petit trou percer a Mémère,*" that means "my little hole pierced." It doesn't mean anything much, but was a term of endearment. My pépère would sit in his rocking chair by the window, or on a warm summer evening on the front porch, and read his western novels by Zane Grey.

Mémère couldn't read or write, but that didn't stop her from doing whatever she wanted, and it seemed to me that she could do anything. When we came to visit, she would make what she called her "George Washington Pie." It was this delicious white cake with strawberry jam and frosting. When we were there visiting on the farm, many local family members and friends would drop in and be invited for dinner. Mémère would have a huge table set for everyone, and of course, that George Washington Pie was for dessert. I remember her coming over and gently putting her hands on my shoulders and whispering to me, "Don't you worry! They ate your cake, but I'll make you another one tomorrow!"

I also remember one morning during our July visit when I was eleven or twelve years old. Mémère had made fresh bread that morning. She must have gotten up at 4:00 or 5:00 a.m. to stoke up that wood stove and bake bread for us. I loved her warm doughy bread, and to top it off there would be fresh strawberries or raspberries and real cream and real butter. Mémère would sit in her seat at the table with a cup of tea and I would sit next to her. She would slice bread for me and watch me eating it with the strawberries and cream.

My mother came downstairs that morning and, of course, she understood better than I did what her mother had gone through to produce that bread for us so early in the morning. She cautioned me, "Don't eat that whole loaf of bread!"

My mémère leaned forward and placed her hand on my arm and said, "Your mother isn't the boss here!"

She then turned to my mother and said in French, *"Tairez vous!"* "You keep quiet now. Let her eat as much as she wants!" Perhaps my mother's bold spirit came from her mother, and I hope I inherited a little bit of it, too.

I've never forgotten that special moment in the warm kitchen with three generations of women: me and my mother and my grandmother. When I look back now, I see the similarities among us. Like her mother before her, my mother loved her time with her grandchildren. She loved having my daughter sit down with her for dinner when she was a toddler, and I'm certain she allowed her to eat as much as she wanted of a delicious treat. Later when she became a widow, she would cook special meals for her teenaged grandson and they would enjoy dinner together once or twice a week. Now, I am Mémère to two amazing little grandsons. I treasure my time with them, in particular, watching these little ones at the dinner table.

Telling this story brings to mind Mémère and Pépère standing on the stoop outside their kitchen door seeing us off, one more time, Mémère wiping her eyes with her handkerchief not knowing if she would ever see us again. I didn't realize the significance of the moment at that time, but it definitely tugs at my heart today.

Elaine Palmer

What Would Aunt Nettie Say?

I have been jogging for the past thirty years as a way to get exercise and enjoy the outdoors. The bridge between my conscious thoughts and my unconscious mind seems to become more fluid while I'm running. Maybe it's the improved blood flow to my brain that creates this phenomenon. Who knows why, but the beneficial outcome is that I have reconnected in spirit with my Aunt Nettie.

While I'm running, my mind may become very active in synchronicity with my moving body or it will just zone out as if I'm meditating. One day, quite randomly, the topic of aunts came up in that space of grey matter. So I started playing little mind games about aunts to pass the miles away.

First, I started to recall each of my aunts' distinctive laughs. That's all it took to get things going! Next, I rated my aunts on their playfulness factor. That was enjoyable because I was able to regress in my running mind to being a young child having enjoyable memory moments with my aunts. Memories were unlocked and the emotional connection in my young life to Aunt Nettie, Aunt Rosy B, and Aunt Rosy P. was re-experienced. Unfortunately, my Aunt Fanny died when I was too young to remember her clearly.

Continuing my jog, I decided to free associate about each aunt separately. What a fun study that was! I recalled their voices and speech patterns, their styles of parenting my cousins, the way they smiled, how they interacted with my parents, phrases that they often used, and so much more. I was reviewing things about each aunt from the perspective of my younger observing self.

The thought process took a more serious shift in another direction with the realization that I am currently about the same age or older than my aunts were in those memories. My child's mind viewed them as strong loving women without problems. I wondered now about their life wisdom and how they confronted challenges. As a child, I wasn't tuned into their day-to-day struggles as a mother, woman, wife, individual, and so on. I bonded with them during holidays and family visits as a young niece. The fifty-six-year-old me today longed for a conversation with my aunts as they were during the 1960s. That was when Aunt Nettie surfaced as the one who wanted to participate in my runs to share her spirit and energy.

My running mind jogged down that side street to figure out why Aunt Nettie was the one to step up! Aunt Nettie was highly respected by my parents and our family in general. Aunt Nettie had advanced awareness abilities for sizing up a situation and sharing spontaneously her bull's eye intuition. Due to all her life experiences and her extensive social network, Aunt Nettie was able to tell a real-life, first-person story to support each of her beliefs. What fun it was to sit at the table and hear the adult conversations flow!

Aunt Nettie's fashion also wowed us. She dressed like a cosmopolitan magazine model. (This pop-up of a related cognition demonstrates how the running mind travels.) Incidentally, I will leap off topic further to mention that Aunt Nettie's black lamb fur coat hangs in my closet on alternating years in a sharing arrangement with my sister.

These thoughts entertain me while I am running with my mind's loose thought structures ping-ponging away to expose whatever wants to surface. On a very deep level, I knew all along that Aunt Nettie emerged as a pseudo-therapist for greater reasons. Aunt Nettie had such a powerful life force because she lived so smartly, kindly, honestly, naturally, and courageously. I experienced her in my world when I was moving from childhood to adolescence and young adulthood. Her influence remains with me.

Stamped in my young mind was the story of Aunt Nettie as a young woman in love with my uncle. Why would my grandfather reject her and cause a feud between himself and his love-smitten only son? Aunt Nettie found ways to circumvent that power play by her future father-in-law. Yes, her mother was divorced in an era when Sicilian families irrationally blamed women for family disappointments. Through her heartache, Aunt Nettie lived beyond that rocky start, married her lover, and found space to love her father-in-law over the decades of shared family times. My running mind is drawn to non-fiction family fairy tales filled with drama!

Aunt Nettie continues to release all of that positive energy to me now so many years after she died. What I do while running is first, allow my mind to think all about Aunt Nettie. I can see her, hear her laugh, remember her style and witness her assertiveness. Next, I pose a situation to her which is usually a personal theme that keeps me stuck or some experience that I'm processing. Finally, I watch her reaction and I listen.

I can hear, in my running mind most clearly, what she would say. I sometimes think that I have appointed her as my personal trainer, my coach, and my therapist. Aunt Nettie hears the challenges or dilemmas that I face and she cares. She talks with me about these issues, and in her characteristic style, she guides me with her infinite strength and wisdom. What's funny is that I can also hear her spunky voice and feel her love while I hear the solutions and warmth that she offers to me. We often laugh together, too.

Sometimes Aunt Nettie is silent. She knows that sometimes what I need is just for her to listen and understand.

Nina Snyder

Skating With Mom

She sees me coming in the door and her face lights up. "Oh, it's you!" Beaming, she draws me closer to her and says, "Why don't I remember that you are so pretty? Your face doesn't have any wrinkles!" And then she muses, "I never was that pretty."

All this comes from the mother who reminded me time and again when I was a child and adolescent, "You will never be pretty. You will look just like me." In a similar vein, she declared to my sister, "You will never be smart like your sister."

Now she is ninety. Her eyes are dim; her expression a bit absent. She totters without her walker; sometimes she stumbles even while holding on to it. Occasionally she surprises me with some acute observation or an assessment of her situation in life, such as, "I am lonely now, but I could do more to interact with the other women here." Or, "I know if I exercise I feel better, but I just don't want to do it." Her reasoning about some things is quite clear and sound: she is adamant about not lingering with any kind of life support or even any emergency treatment, and she wishes to be generous and give gifts to her grandchildren while she's alive to do it. I help her understand how generous she can afford to be. She was upset about the recent earthquake in Haiti, and asked me to make a contribution for her to the recovery. At the same time, she forgets much, and her brain now struggles not only with the recent past, but with old memories, as well. She forgets which great-grandchildren belong to which grandchild, whether it is afternoon or evening, if James or Nora or Thomas has called her lately, and just how much that "lottery winning" (i.e., her long-term insurance policy) is paying her. She asks, "Now how old am I?" "Did I really live in Virginia?" With some prompting, I believe she really does remember. We make myriad journeys into her past when I visit her or talk with her on the phone.

One great benefit of memory loss is that it seems to help her reconstruct her life in a much kinder light than reality would have it. Dad never really drank THAT much. Her childhood was one happy incident after the other ... no hardships, no beatings, and no social stigma worth mentioning vis a vis her parents' immigrant status. She forgets how she resented my father's affection for me and how she spurned my achievements, seeing them mostly in the light of how different my opportunities were from hers. I suppose it's just as well that she forgets all that.

Before I fully appreciated how much of what she forgets and doesn't understand is a result of brain damage, I would try to correct her and reason with her. I'm getting much better at simply accepting it, letting it be what she wants it to be. I do get upset occasionally, taking it as a criticism of me, for example, when she tells my sons that she is terribly lonely. I know she has far more social interaction now than she had had in Florida for the last several years she was there alone. She only remembers the years she was still very active in her church and with substitute teaching in the public schools. She forgets the last years, when she couldn't drive; couldn't manage her medications, couldn't keep her house and her person clean and neat; didn't pay her bills on time; and squandered thousands of dollars on bogus sweepstakes and lotteries.

So, I have a daily phone conversation and two or three visits a week with this complex, confounding, somewhat disheveled, often confused woman who is my mother. She loves me, as she tells me daily. I am no longer a rival, an impediment to her own achievements, someone to dominate or, failing that, to humiliate. I cannot forget the evening I took her to a meeting of an organization to which I belonged in my forties. When two prominent women who had taken me under their wings, urging me to take leadership roles in the community, remarked to my mother that she must be quite proud of me, she replied, "Well, yes, Jane is talented, but, you know, she can be a little 'smart around the mouth!'" She seemed a very foolish, bitter, and ill-bred sixty-something woman, and I was utterly embarrassed. Now, no longer a threat, I am the angel who looks after her.

I manage her affairs and pay her bills. I plan her care with the management of the assisted living facility where she lives. I discuss her needs with the staff, and trouble-shoot when she cannot represent her needs by herself (most of the time). I go through her closet and drawers and take out the soiled clothes and put them in her laundry basket. I find her pajamas in the drawer when she insists they have been stolen. I meet with her doctors to review her care needs and see that they fill out the forms we need to file for her insurance. I take her to appointments with specialists. We shop for Kleenex and hose and hair spray. When I take her places, I put her coat on her, tie the belt, put on her hat and gloves, buckle her into the car, and stow her walker in the trunk. I reverse the process when we get to where we are going, and again when we leave to go back to her place. Returned, I hang her coat in the closet, put away her hat and gloves and help her into bed—she is always exhausted when we return, whether it's from an appointment, a visit to my home, a shopping trip, or even a lunch out. She sometimes sighs, "I guess I'm your baby now," when I get her ready and buckle her in. She thanks me. Again and again. The woman, who when I was a child and had a fever blister would say to me, "It is the bad coming out of you," and who just a few years ago yelled at me, "You don't have a kind bone in your body!" now tells me daily how good I am.

The most bittersweet aspect of our relationship is this: she often tells me things like, "Everyone should be lucky enough to have a daughter like you." Invariably, then, she will say something like, "You deserve to have a daughter, and you don't." She remembers the life and death of my daughter, and she will say something like, "I'm so sorry she died. I remember her." She does indeed remember her. She remembers details like her "spindly legs" and gentle little giggle; the hope we had on her first birthday that maybe she would make it after all; and seeing her the day before she died. She remembers, and she says to me, "She was so sick and weak. I am so very sorry that you lost her. You deserve a good daughter like you are to me."

So here I am, thrown together with this woman with whom I have had a tortured emotional relationship most of my life, whose dependence on me is great and wearing, with whom I have never shared any intimacy, even my overwhelming grief over the loss of my daughter. Here she is, now perhaps the person who imagines best, even with her demented mind, how great that loss still is and will be to me always. She knows what a good daughter means to an old, confused, lonely mother. And so, I guess, do I.

I try to keep in mind what I should celebrate about my mother. Given her humble beginnings, she made much of her life. She is very intelligent, and she applied that intelligence well, earning a bachelors' degree in three years, graduating first in her class at the local teacher's college the year I finished my sophomore year in high school. She did it primarily because she wanted a better job than working at a department store in order to send us to good colleges. Education was a primary concern in the family, with my parents recognizing that they had academically talented children and wanting to support their educations.

Mother was intellectually curious. We had encyclopedias, and Mom was always looking up something. We took educational trips to Washington, Williamsburg, Canada, and more... places we could drive to, staying in what were then called "guest houses," the B&Bs of the fifties. She had a real desire to grow beyond the small coal town where she was born, and she grew with us, excited by each new venture out into the world. Her mind was open, and she continued to evolve well into her seventies.

I also admire my mother's work ethic. She brought great energy to her many undertakings: excelling in college and as an elementary school teacher, going to graduate school and becoming a fine principal, substitute teaching in Florida until she was eighty-four, and always doing the home repairs, lawn work, gardening, canning, and furniture upholstering. You name the job, and she could do it and do it well!

So, I respect my mother for her many natural talents, her work ethic, her curiosity, her achievements, her kindness to strangers, her concern for others, and, above all, her love and support for my sons. Yet the legacy of hurt and rejection is not easily set aside.

With sixty-eight years of conflicting messages and memories roiling in my head, what I am able to do is grit my teeth when she yells at me for not believing her possessions have been stolen, to bite my tongue when she returns to type and is sharp or nasty, and to try not to become bitter about being responsible for a woman who did not provide the love and security for which I often yearned. Oddly enough—perhaps because she did, after all, give me life; and perhaps because she is so often eager now to express appreciation; and perhaps because I retain some deeply hidden memories of her as a kinder, more supportive and loving mother; and perhaps because I do recall her acts of generosity; and, finally, because she has been a very, very good grandmother to my sons – I find I am, indeed, devoted to her. I do what I can to make her happy, taking her for rides in the countryside that give her such pleasure, helping her remember the good parts of her past, letting her see my "wrinkle-free" face smiling at her, and, when I find her depressed because she's lost her teeth again, or soiled her bedclothes, or misses my father, encouraging her to snap out of it. I appeal to her still-intact sense of humor with the likes of, "Come on, Mary, put on your roller skates and let's go out for some lunch!" She replies, "Okay, as long as you get me back in time for my tap-dancing lessons!"

Jane Richards

Savings

"Every time your father decides to purchase new labor saving inventions, he has to work harder and longer to earn the money to pay for them. Something is not right."

Mother Cora was resting with her feet up while I re-arranged the farmhouse kitchen that had been transformed this morning to a laundry room.

On his way from bed to barn in the morning darkness of a Minnesota winter, Dad had wrestled the new Maytag washer over the doorsill between outdoor storage and kitchen and placed extra kettles of soft water on the stove top to supplement the reservoir on the cook stove. I had stoked the fire, cleaned out the wood ashes, adjusted drafts, installed the flexible exhaust hose to the kick-start gasoline engine on the Maytag, filled the fuel tank, and placed two galvanized rinse tubs on a bench in reach of the swinging power-wringer. Then I hurried off to help finish the milking while Mom prepared breakfast and kept the wood fire roaring to heat the water for Monday wash day. With morning chores finished, Dad, Sister Ruth, and I were off for school in the Ford leaving Mom, Sister June, and Baby Lois to launder the clothing and sheets and hang them to dry on the permanent outdoor lines beside the house.

Mother Cora's farm, 1939.

Now the winter school day was over, early darkness with kerosene lamps was soon to be a handicap and I was helping to return the kitchen to its primary purpose. Exhaustion marked her face. She felt fortunate to have the only modern, power washing machine in the community. It did clean clothing and sheets without resort to backbreaking washboard and plunger, but her face told me it still had been a punishing day for a farm housewife.

As I emptied tubs and stored equipment, she listed recent purchases to save labor: the gasoline engine water pump to cool the cream, the gravity tank to furnish water for the cows' drinking cups, the new cream separator, the new concrete floor for the barn, the cistern to save rainwater for laundry, and the Model T for travel to teaching jobs at distant country schools. The year was 1924 when I was eleven years old and Mom was concerned that Dad was working too hard to pay for her new washing machine. I knew she was worried about saving dollars for my high school one day soon, but today that was not on her list.

My mom Cora, what a woman!

Paul W. Bixby

Until You Got Here

I am descended from Pennsylvania Dutch women who shun doctors for a daily regimen of hard work and a starchy diet. Not counting my birth, my mother has been hospitalized only twice in my forty-three years.

"Pokey got into a polecat," my father shouted from the basement as I entered the house after school. Tearing down the stairs, I saw my father and grandmother bent over our dog, drenched and standing knee deep in tomato juice. Empty jars rolled underfoot as they doused her in a large tub that usually held winter potatoes. Pokey shook and trembled like a horse attempting to shed a biting fly. Seeing me, the dog launched herself over the tub's rim, escaping up the stairs.

"We were doing fine until you got here," my grandmother chuckled, pausing for a moment to listen as Pokey clattered around the dining room above us, then she stooped to gather the quart jars. Three had broken in the struggle and Mom's hard work during the heat of August would get poured down the drain. "Let's not worry your mother with this until she's home from the hospital and feeling better," she said, giving me her two-eyed wink. I nodded, racing up the stairs after Pokey. As I pursued her throughout the house, I laughed for the first time since my mother's hysterectomy. Even at eleven I knew this meant I would remain her youngest child.

Thirty years later, I nearly dropped the phone when my father called to say, "Your mother might have had a heart attack. How quickly can you get here?" When I arrived at her hospital room, the bed was empty with Dad asleep in the visitor's chair. For a second, I could not bear to wake him, searching the room for any sign that my mother was still alive. Dad stirred and opened his eyes, speaking as if I had been there all along, "She's been taken for tests. Let's get some coffee."

My father filled me in on the events of the past few hours. Listening, I focused on the brown spots that freckled the backs of his hands. In my mind's eye I pictured him, muscular and youthful, holding Pokey beneath a torrent of tomato juice. Five times he repeated, "She couldn't get her breath." Finishing, we took the elevator back to her room and I held my own breath, recalling the sweet-sour odor of skunk and tomatoes. I followed him through the door. Her bed was still empty.

"Dad, I'm going to see what's going on."

After finally speaking with the nurse at the station, I returned to her room. My mother was in bed, describing something to my father as he attempted to adjust her bed. Bending, I held her and we both started to cry, something unusual and scary for us. When I pulled away, she said, "I was fine until you got here." Laughter erased our tears.

Beth McLaughlin

Je Suis Mama

I'm nine years old and I absolutely, positively, without a doubt, refuse to gargle. My mother, a registered nurse, is holding a glass of salty water in one hand and a thermometer in the other. I'm not the kind of kid who typically defies authority, but I feel miserable and have every intention of seriously milking the situation. She tilts her head of wavy red hair, and her blue eyes gently plead for compliance. I feel a little sorry for her but not enough to surrender. She means well, but I see no way for me to fling my head back with a mouthful of that stinging concoction without choking.

Mom has already tried the informative approach, telling me how much better my raw throat will feel. I respond with stony silence. She demonstrates with a sample gargle of her own, which is entertaining but unconvincing. She even tries to barter: a gargle for an episode of "Hawaii 5-0." I honk my stuffy nose into a Puff's and she gives up the fight. I find the victory quite satisfying. She smiles and I know I'm still loved when she offers to bring me some ice cream. She just wants to take my temperature first, and I am happy to give her this little pleasure. I always enjoy watching Mom skillfully snap the sliver of mercury down the thin reed of glass. She gently places it under my tongue, holds my wrist, and checks her watch. I don't know what it all means but I cherish the ritual.

Suddenly, Mom jerks the thermometer from my lips. "What have I done?" she wails. "This is Lovey's thermometer!"

I'm overwhelmed with disgust – dog germs! Pttttuuey! I know I'll be dead in minutes.

There's no time to waste and she hurries me from the bed as I feel myself gagging reflexively. She puts the glass in my hand. "Quick. Take this. Swirl it around, swish it way back in your throat, and spit it out."
I repeat the swirl-swish-spit mantra until the glass is drained and I'm exhausted by my efforts. She helps me back into bed and plumps my pillows. She looks perplexed. "Oh, silly me," she sighs. "I was wrong. This is the right thermometer. Oh, well, that gargling won't hurt you any. Now, how about that ice cream?"

It is years later, and I'm twenty years old, a savvy college sophomore. I open a beautiful Valentine's Day card from my parents. My mother has written a long note on the back and much to my surprise, it's in a foreign language. She had never told me of this talent!

I give it to the girl in the next room who majors in French. She reads it silently, jotting the translation into English. She sighs. "This is deep. The meaning is profound. Your mother is amazing."

I read the words aloud and must admit I don't thoroughly understand it but I'm not about to show my ignorance. Philosophy is not my strong point.

My roommate, eyes closed, nods her head in reverent appreciation. "Don't you see? She's giving you life's wisdom. I wish I had a groovy mother like that."

I phoned Mom, thanking her for her lovely words. I told her how I was the envy of my dorm as the card was passed from room to room. Through the muffled silence at the end of the line, I swear I could see her face contorted with delight. She had randomly pulled out words from a French dictionary and tossed them on the page without rhyme or reason.

I'm fifty years old. Mom is seventy-seven and still dishing up her special brand of life's wisdom in the grooviest way.

Kimberly Townsend

About the Contributors

Claire Aldrich works in the financial world by day. She lives in Upper Westchester, New York, loves the country, and has nourished her love of creative writing over many years. She also writes poetry.

Elizabeth Ashe earned an MFA in Creative Writing from Chatham University. She was an Assistant Editor for The Fourth River. She currently spends her time between Tacoma, Chicago, and Pittsburgh. When not traveling or writing, Ashe is a visual artist.

Michael Azevedo has been a writer and producer of print, interactive, online, and broadcast television content for more than fifteen years. A father of two children, he resides in Massachusetts.

Gabeba Baderoon is a poet and teacher. She is the recipient of the DaimlerChrysler Award for South African Poetry 2005. Among her publications are A Hundred Silences and The Dream in the Next Body. She lives in Pennsylvania with her partner and three cats.

For the last thirty-five years, **John Bellanti** has been a psychotherapist in private practice as well as a life coach. He lives in State College, Pennsylvania with his wife, Carolyn. They spend much time interacting with international students helping them develop their gifts and feel appreciated in this country. They have three grown children and five grandchildren.

Marina Berges is a kindergarten teacher and nanny who has been working with children for the past forty years. In 1997, her mother passed away, but left an impression on her with her eternal optimism. Marina admired that quality in her mother and lives by it every day. She has two sons and three grandchildren and resides in Pepperell, Massachusetts.

Paul W. Bixby is a retired nonagenarian university administrator and professor. Among other writing projects he has prepared a series of short event-stories for a target readership of great-grandchildren.

Suzanne (Sica) Bokenko is a dedicated ARMY wife and a mother of three beautiful girls. She has served her country in the U.S. Army and is now an ASCP (MT)-certified Medical Technologist working in the fields of Microbiology/Immunology and Laboratory Information Systems as a Department of Defense Civilian employee. She also holds a Master's Degree in Hospital Administration.

Susan Bordo holds the Otis A. Singletary Chair in Humanities at the University of Kentucky and is the author of many critically acclaimed, highly influential books and articles, including Unbearable Weight: Feminism, Western Culture and the Body. Bordo's writing has been translated into many languages. She is a popular campus lecturer on topics such eating disorders, cosmetic surgery, the male body, racism and the body, the impact of contemporary media, and adoption.

Roslynne Canfield has been an office manager in the marine industry for thirty years. She has three children, nine grandchildren, and one great granddaughter. After living in New York for most of her life, she moved to Scituate, Massachusetts nine years ago where she still enjoys playing Scrabble. She also volunteers at the local library and enjoys reading, walking, and spending time with family.

Cindy Carubia has been an elementary school teacher for seventeen years in the beautiful mountains of the Hudson Valley, New York, where she works to engage children in becoming passionate readers and writers and budding environmentalists. She enjoys hikes in the mountains with her husband Mike, and sweet cavalier, Riley. She loves watching her children Dayna and Danny become who they were meant to be.

Josephine Carubia is a writer, educator, consultant, mother of two, and grandmother of six. A former editor of non-fiction books in New York City, she holds a Ph.D. in literature from Fordham University and was formerly Chief Academic Liaison Officer for the Penn State College of Medicine. She lives in Pennsylvania.

Jane Cash is a high-tech homecare nurse living on Long Island, New York. Married for forty-six years, mother of three, grandmother of eight, and ambulance volunteer EMT-CC for more than twenty years.

Alice Clark is the coordinator of volunteer services at Mount Nittany Medical Center in State College, Pennsylvania. She is an avid photographer and hiker. She is also a member of two book clubs, one of which has twelve members from different countries (Brazil, China, Colombia, Czech Republic, Germany, Hungary, India, Iran, Japan, Malaysia, Mexico, Norway, S. Korea, Taiwan, Turkey, and the U.S.).

Rebecca Clever is a professional writer, musician, and graduate of Chatham University's MFA in Creative Writing program. She serves as editor/publisher of the independent on-line literary journal, Blast Furnace. Her work has appeared in several journals, Split Oak Press' anthology, One for the Road, and two Magnapoets anthologies. A lifelong resident of Pittsburgh, Pennsylvania, she works in the healthcare technology industry.

Annette Conklin is a classical pianist and retired music teacher living with her husband Dick in Saint Paul, Minnesota. She adjudicates piano students state-wide and nationally, and currently administers a pre-college chamber music competition in partnership with The Saint Paul Chamber Orchestra. For fun, she enjoys reading, traveling, good wine, theater and concerts, The New York Times crossword puzzles, and cooking pots of food for guests.

Richard Conklin grew up in southwest Minneapolis and after earning baccalaureate and graduate degrees in English and American literature began a career as a reporter. He subsequently returned to campus, spending almost four decades in university administration, specializing in communications and public relations before retiring in 2001.

Lisa Luddy-Courcy, RNC, MSN, C-EFM, is an Assistant Professor of Nursing at Endicott College in Beverly, Massachusetts. The mother of three grown daughters, she plans to continue playing baseball into her golden years. She resides in Taunton, Massachusetts with her husband of thirty-five years.

Connie Cousins is a retired widow who spent forty years as a Certified Registered Nurse Anesthetist and moved to State College, Pennsylvania in 2008. She writes a weekly column for the Centre Daily Times and is hoping to do more writing for magazines and inspirational booklets.

Joseph D'Ambrosio is a retired engineer and adventurer pursuing life and truth. He shares life with three children, four grandchildren, a large growing family, and friends.

Laura de Kreij specializes in sustainable development at a Fortune 500 company in Geneva, Switzerland. She enjoys life at the foot of the Alps with her husband and daughter.

Christy Diulus is the editor of Chatham University's literary journal, The Fourth River, and has been on staff since 2004. Her fiction has recently appeared in Paradigm and SNReview. She also teaches English at the Community College of Allegheny County and works at the Carnegie Library of Pittsburgh.

Fritz Eckert is a retired teacher who has found satisfaction in expressing himself through photography, but nurtures a lifelong passion for the written word.

Sally Eckert is an occupational therapist who likes reading, cooking, knitting, genealogy, and watching her amazing children negotiate new phases of their lives. She and her husband, Fritz, enjoy lakeside living in North Carolina.

Douglas Glorie is an environmental engineer who lives in Montclair, New Jersey with his wife and two adventurous daughters. He enjoys food, traveling, and spending time with family and friends.

Joanne Balmer Green enjoys a fulfilling professional life working with her husband as a researcher in nutritional sciences at Penn State University; scientific writing has always come easily for her. She also volunteers for several organizations, became a mother late in life, and has always nurtured the creative streak and love for family traditions that she inherited from her own mom.

Hoasua is a pseudonym. She lives and works in Vietnam.

Robert Innis is Professor of Philosophy at the University of Massachusetts Lowell. He has written in many formats about meanings in life.

Hattie Mae Johnson recalls a fabulous childhood near Columbus, Mississippi. She graduated from Mississippi State College for Women in 1939 and was happily married to Roger Johnson for sixty-three years. They were blessed with five children, eleven grandchildren, and three great grandchildren. She currently resides in Hattiesburg, Mississippi.

Mizuho Kawasaki (川崎みずほ in Japanese) was born in Tokyo, Japan. She lives in State College, Pennsylvania with her husband and two children. She enjoys American culture through sewing costumes and knitting Gryffindor mufflers for Halloween and quilting, cooking, and reading.

Shel Julian Kessel still gets ink on her hands while working on her Ph.D. in education at Ohio State University. She also, from time to time, gets flour on her hands when she struggles to bake cookies without burning them or making a kitchen-wide mess.

Hyo Kim is Publisher and Chief Executive Officer of The Korea Canada Central Daily and Arirang Korea TV.

Kyung Ryoon Kim is a jewelry designer in Toronto, Canada.

Petya Kirilova-Grady is Director of Volunteer Services at The Crisis Center in Memphis, Tennessee. Her blog How To Marry A Bulgarian (www.howtomarryabulgarian.com) is an on-going story about bi-cultural marriage. Her husband Kyle is her most favorite character.

Andrea Pinto Lebowitz is Professor Emerita after thirty-six years as a professor in English Literature and Women's Studies at Simon Fraser University in BC, Canada. Her publications reflect a lifelong interest in literature and nature. Her mother, Anne Pinto, born in 1910, was an early influence on the importance of gardens.

Joyce Maroney is an enthusiastic mother, wife, quilter, and community volunteer. She works as a high-technology marketing executive in the Boston area.

Liz Maroney currently finds herself in Arlington, Virginia, but has lived in New York, London, and Washington, DC itself – though she will always be a Boston girl at heart. She works at Rebuilding Together, a desk-bound idealist trying to leave the world that little bit better than she found it.

Victoria Tilney McDonough writes about what makes people tick and why. Her interviews with people have varied from actor John Cusack and writer Stephen King to the late Jerry Rubin of the Chicago Seven and the Central Park Jogger. Victoria lives in Alexandria, Virginia with her amazing husband, two delicious boys, and ebullient dog Noodle.

Beth McLaughlin earned an MFA in Creative Writing from Goddard College in 2006. Since then, she's been blessed to be able to write full-time and is currently working on two novels.

Kim McNamara lives with her husband, son, and cat in London, Ontario. She works in the life insurance industry but dreams about writing from her home office one day.

Rebecca Suzanne Miller has an MFA in Creative Writing, teaches Composition and Literature in northwest Ohio, and is a movie buff. She lives with her beagle/dachshund mix, Ruby, and exalts the amazing women in her life for their tireless love and inspiration.

Alyce Moore is a general counsel for a large software company. She is married and has two children. She lives with her husband John and their yellow lab, Pete.

Anna Marie Nachman works at Penn State University, is the mother of five, and lives in Rolling Stone, Pennsylvania. She is a singer and enjoys cooking and entertaining family and friends.

Elaine Palmer lives in Fitchburg, Massachusetts with her husband of forty-five years. Now retired, she loves spending time with her two young grandsons and enjoys the time to pursue her hobbies of knitting, needlework, and reading.

Michele Glorie Palmer is a mother of two and corporate communications director of a large software company. She grew up on a farm in New York; spent her early thirties living in New York City; and now lives in what she believes is one of the quaintest towns in New England. Her mother, Jo Carubia, is her day-to-day source of inspiration.

Ann Seltzer Pangborn lives in State College, Pennsylvania. She is an artist, working primarily as a feltmaker and as an Expressive Arts Therapist.

Alpa M. Patel lives in Manhattan with her husband and son. She is a budding writer and blogs at ampostscript.blogspot.com.

Kirti Patel is a physician, writer, and blogger who lives with her husband and two children in Massachusetts. You may find more of her writing at ktheblogger.blogspot.com.

Laurie Mansell Reich holds an MFA in Writing from Chatham University and lives in Kittanning, Pennsylvania with her husband, three German Shepherds, and two zebra finches. She is a freelance writer and copyeditor with passions for reading and gardening.

Jane Richards is a pseudonym. She and her husband are both working on memoirs for their three sons and eight grandchildren. She holds AB and Ph.D. degrees and is retired from a university position.

Millie Santana lives in Danvers, Massachusetts with her two children and their cat Don Quijote. Mom and brother live in Hialeah, Florida. Mom's pastime is doing jigsaw puzzles with more than one thousand pieces and using the internet (we call her cyber grandma!); Francisco's is listening to music and watching TV.

Ela Sikora lives in State College, Pennsylvania with her husband and two children; she does research on development of new materials for medical implants. She loves to read, cook, run, and swim.

Juliet Silveri is a former book production and freelance editor. She resides in Groton, Massachusetts with her husband and two children, where she indulges her love of gardening.

Marilyn Silverman is a psychotherapist in private practice in Wilton, Connecticut. She is the editor of the newsletter for the Connecticut Society of Psychoanalytic Psychology and is presently working on a paper that addresses the current uses of the concepts of dissociation and anxiety.

Nina Snyder is a high school crisis counselor in the Hudson River Valley. She is also an artist, currently passionate about creating miniature paintings. She owns and manages an antiques store in the historic village of Montgomery, New York. Her family and friends have cheered each time she crossed the finish line of the New York Marathon.

Taryn Snyder is completing her M.A. in Elementary Special Education while working in a first grade classroom in Boston. She volunteers outside of the classroom with the National Pancreas Foundation. When her schedule allows, Taryn enjoys baking, trying new restaurants, and spending time with family and friends.

Laura Shea Souza is a public relations practitioner and writer. She lives in Stow, Massachusetts with her husband and two beautiful daughters.

Kate Staley is a child psychologist who works mostly with college students. She is married to a ceramic artist and is the mother of two teenage girls. She has written for regional magazines on topics as diverse as gifted education, child obesity, workforce development, and shaken baby syndrome. Her family's next sabbatical is approaching and she looks forward to more adventures.

Darlene A. Throckmorton is a retired advertising executive living in Pine Groves Mills, Pennsylvania. She is an avid gardener, an inveterate hiker, and an artisan baker of local renown.

Kimberly Townsend lives in a lovely Pennsylvania town, where her parents, friends, and cats are a constant source of joy and amusement. She teaches, counsels, and advocates on behalf of victims of domestic violence, and volunteers with the rehabilitation of injured and orphaned wildlife.

Nancy Tuana is the DuPont/Class of 1949 Professor of Philosophy and founding Director of the Rock Ethics Institute at Penn State University. She is the author of numerous books and articles in the area of feminist philosophy. She is the proud mother of two boys who are on the verge of becoming men and she is grateful for the close bond between them and her own parents.

Sinem Turgut is from Turkey. She has lived in State College, Pennsylvania with her husband since 2007. She is soon to graduate from Penn State University with an MBA degree. Sinem loves to read, cook, and travel.

Elizabeth Vozzola is a professor of Psychology at Saint Joseph College in West Hartford, Connecticut. She is an avid reader of fiction, memoir, and biography whose scholarly interests center on moral development and women's development.

Nancy Werlin is the author of several young adult novels, including The New York Times bestseller Impossible, the National Book Award finalist The Rules of Survival, and the Edgar award-winning mystery The Killer's Cousin, and her most recent novel, Extraordinary. Visit her website at www.nancywerlin.com.

Anne Allan Whitney lives on a small farm in central Pennsylvania with her husband and four dogs. Her horses are her teachers and she dreams of dancing with them under the full moon.